Valley Studio

More Than a Place

E. Reid Gilbert and Jef Lambdin

Valley Studio: More Than a Place

Published by Wheatmark®
1760 East River Road, Suite 145, Tucson, Arizona 85718 USA
www.wheatmark.com

ISBN: 978-1-62787-396-3
LCCN: 2016934874

When words are not enough there is music.
When music is insufficient there is silence.

CONTENTS

Death
204 is
More

Foreword

There is little I can say to prepare either the committed or the casual reader for the lives expressed in these pages. I have taken the liberty to adopt for this collection Grant Bashore's title of his personal story: MORE THEN A PLACE. That theme seems to be included in each of these reminiscences . . . certainly in mine.

I have attempted to put these stories in a loose chronology, even though each recollection stands on its own. There are many repetitions . . .sometimes even contradictions of events, which I let stand. It's like the five blind men who attempted to describe an elephant . . ..each of course was reporting on the part he was experiencing in his own personal sense of touch.

I'm not suggesting that any blindness was involved. Here we celebrate the individual perspective each person brought to Valley Studio and how the experiences were taken into their subsequent lives and work. A bit of editing occurred such as when one person remembered the Wyoming Valley as Bear Valley.

It should also be noted that I'm discovering things now, completely unaware to me at that time. I hope the writers will forgive me for adding an occasional addendum, not to correct the story, but to add a clarifying item or nuance to them.

Reid Gilbert

Valley Studio

Jef Lambdin

In the 1970s one could study movement theater at many studios and colleges throughout the United States. Carlo Mazzone-Clementi had his Dell Arte School of Mime & Comedy in Blue Lake, CA. Jewel Walker, Moni Yakim, Bob Francesconi, James Donlon, Bari Rolfe and others were teaching at universities. Samuel Avital had his Le Centre du Silence in Boulder, CO; C.W. Metcalf his Magic Mountain Mime School in Tallahassee, FL; and Tony Montanaro shared his work at his Celebration Mime Theater in South Paris, ME.

When one considers all of the movement theater training offered at that time, one studio stands out— The Valley Studio in Spring Green, Wisconsin. This hub of movement theater exploration was the brainchild, passion and vision of E. Reid Gilbert. From 1970 through 1979, the Valley Studio blossomed in the Wyoming Valley of Wisconsin, seven miles south of Spring Green and forty miles west of Madison. From a small beginning mime class in a barn, the Studio grew to include three main facets: year-round instruction; summer workshops by master teachers such as Mamako Yoneyama, Ken Feit, William Burdick, Hovey & Judy Burgess, Jacques Burdick, Peter Hoff, Carlo Mazzone-Clementi and Tom Leabhart; as well as a touring performing arts troupe—The Wisconsin Mime Company which was later to be known as the Wisconsin Mime Theatre.

Valley Studio 1972. Photo by David Herwaldt.

HOW IT ALL STARTED

According to Reid Gilbert, "In 1969, I brought several of my Lambuth College theatre students to participate in the Uplands Arts Council's summer program, mounting several productions in the Gard Theatre in Spring Green. That year my family and I stayed in the Spring Green area for me to finish my doctoral dissertation at the University of Wisconsin. The next spring, a new friend of ours, Dr. Dean Connors, asked me if I could use part of his house to teach mime to his daughter, Susan, and his house boy, Ben Rogner. He had secured the architectural services of Herbert Fritz, an associate of Frank Lloyd Wright, to design an upgrade of an old house and barn on the small Newton Farm on the Upper Wyoming Road. The barn loft provided an excellent studio space for mime instruction. That autumn, Ben and I began occasional performances on the road. The next spring Dr. Connors said that the commute to Madison every day for his work in St. Mary s Hospital was too onerous for him, so he suggested that I invite more students that summer and to use the whole facility."

EARLY '70S GROWTH AND EXPANSION

Into this mix came Barbara Leigh (Co-Founder and Artistic/ Producing Director of the Milwaukee Public Theatre). According to Barbara, "I was at the University of Wisconsin in Madison, working on my dissertation about Jacques Copeau's Theatre du Vieux-Columbier. While working, I realized that mime was kind of the origin of the training so I began searching for a mime class. Of course, what surfaced in Paul's Book Store in Madison was a little notice about Reid Gilbert doing a mime show at some church. I'm like, 'Oh my God, I have to go to this.' So I went to the show and I thought 'This is so fabulous. I want to do this.' So of course Reid was offering mime classes, and I took the classes and just totally fell in love with the art form. Reid invited me to come out to the Studio. I started working at the Studio. Gradually I started working more and more with Reid, and we formed a duo. We traveled all over the state giving performances. I became the Associate Director, and it went from there."

REID GILBERT BEFORE

Now Reid was no stranger to theater and particularly to what we today call Movement Theater. He'd studied Modern Dance with Charles Weidman in 1958, Mime with Etienne Decroux in 1959, and Japanese Noh with Sidayo Kita in 1964. He'd been a Visiting Lecturer in Mime at the National School of Drama in New Delhi, India, in 1965–66. He had received an STM in Religious Drama from Union Theological Seminary in 1963 and completed his Ph.D. in Theatre at the University of Wisconsin just as he was beginning the Valley Studio. So he brought all of this training and experience to bear as he created the Valley Studio.

Speaking of Reid Gilbert, Barbara Leigh offers, "One of the things that really drew me to Reid was the way that he taught mime. It was the whole concept of respect. He talked about how the word "respect" came from the Latin spectare "to look", re "again":

Reid at desk

to keep looking again and again. That concept has been a beacon for me." Tom Leabhart (Professor of Theatre and Resident Artist at Pomona College in Claremont, CA) adds, "Speaking of what Reid brought to all of this, well Reid had this wonderful country kind of wise, sort of like an old country doctor, or old country judge who was there dispensing his wisdom. He believed in the whole person, that everybody should do chores. So we all took on chores. The spirit that Reid brought is exemplified in his wanting to call the little performances 'Sharings.' That's a very Reid kind of thing."

John Towsen (Author of the book *Clowns*, Professor at Bloomfield College and blogmaster extraordinaire of All Fall Down: the Art & Craft of Physical Comedy) recalls, "One thing about Reid was that he was so very open to everything. He took to heart Mao Tse Tung's phrase when he said, 'Let a thousand flowers blossom.' Terry Kerr (Education Director, Children's Theatre of Madison) observes, "He was very open to all kinds of disciplines. I loved that about Reid. We'd experience something and then try to realize it in whatever fashion seemed appropriate; whether it was a spoken piece, a mime piece, a dance piece, a silent theatre piece, or not."

Ronlin Foreman (School Director of the Dell Arte International School of Physical Theatre in Blue Lake, CA) remembers, "It was Reid's conviction concerning Community that set the tone and the atmosphere of the Valley Studio. He believed that it was an artist's personal responsibility for caring for the place—including regard for and maintenance of the studios, preparing meals, conserving resources, as well as being self reliant and collegial. Reid emphasized that the Artist/Performer must be a responsive citizen of the world. Studying there meant a commitment to contribute to the community that sustained the place."

THE WISCONSIN MIME COMPANY/THEATRE

In the early '70s Reid Gilbert and Barbara Leigh, as the Wisconsin Mime Company, shared performances at schools, colleges and arts venues. Barbara Leigh stated, "We were the beginning of the Wisconsin Mime Theater. Actually during the summers the students from the studio became part of the troupe as well. It had all kinds of people in it. But during the year, just the two of us were touring." As you can see from the following list, during these early years many performances and residencies were in Wisconsin, but the Company did work throughout the Midwest including workshops and performances at: Wisconsin State University in River Falls; Viterbo College in Racine, WI; University of Wisconsin, Madison; St. Lawrence Seminary in Mt. Calvary, WI; Mercy College in Detroit, MI; Flambeau High School in Tony, WI; and Waunakee Elementary School in Waunakee, WI.

Barbara Leigh left the Valley Studio in 1974 to form her own company, Friends Mime Theatre. As Leigh was leaving, other performers joined the company. This would prove to be the model for the company over the years as company members would join, contribute, and move on. Even Reid's relationship with the troupe would eventually change, "After a while, I didn't perform with the company. When Tom came in 1976, I backed out a little bit. I got more involved with the administration of the Studio, etc."

According to Terry Kerr, in 1974 and '75, "There were five of us. It was Johnny Aden, me, Kay Doobie Potter, Susan Chrietzberg, and Reid. For the couple of years while I was there we did hundreds of school residencies. We would go out and do workshops and then perform at the end of the day for school assemblies. That was really kind of our bread and butter. We had a longer touring show that we did with all five of us, so we had duets and solos as well as some pieces that included the entire company. We even had some pieces that were just the four of us without Reid. We had a pretty collaborative approach. Pretty much we each composed our own work and then Reid would act as the director. He'd give suggestions and influence the work." Reid Gilbert adds, "We did the booking ourselves. I did it, and then we got Nina Edming, who was running the office."

For an idea of the company's performances during this era, check out this program.

In 1976, Reid wrote to Tom Leabhart to invite him to work at the Valley Studio. According to Leabhart, "How this all happened was I was at the Mime Festival in Viterbo, WI (the International Mime Festival and Institute held at Viterbo College in LaCrosse, WI, in the summer of 1974). I met Reid at the Viterbo Festival. I went there from teaching at the University of Arkansas. There in Wisconsin I saw Jacques Lecoq perform for the first time, and I saw these wonderful dark clowns from Eastern Europe. So that gave me the idea tha I wanted to go there and see what other work was going on. So when I got back to Arkansas, I applied for a grant, which I got. So I went to Poland for three months and Czechoslovakia for two months. While Sally, my wife, and I were in Poland we got a letter from Reid. It said, 'Would you like to come here to the Valley Studio?'

"So Sally and I talked about it. We were young. I mean the University of Arkansas was my first job, so the Valley Studio was only my second job. I went back to University of Arkansas, looked around and said, I'm ready for a change. So there were these negotiations with Reid to bring with me some members of the mime troupe already at the University of Arkansas. I don't remember exactly how many of them finally came to the Valley Studio, but there were Robert Sucher, Susana Hackett, Meg Partridge, Karen Flaherty—I don't remember the exact number, but there were five or six."

As mentioned earlier, it was at this point that Reid stopped performing with the troupe. With Leabhart at the helm and the addition of the new members, the Wisconsin Mime Company changed its name to The Wisconsin Mime Theatre and expanded its repertoire to add corporeal mime. Tom Leabhart notes, "We had a kind of a mixing of genres. Some of the pieces were more clown pieces, and then others were more corporeal mime pieces. We mixed them together." Karen Flaherty (former company member who is now retired and lives in New York City) adds, "We opened the eyes of a lot of people because we would do things with words. One of the works was from a piece, a play called, *Three Sisters Who Are Not Sisters* by Gertrude Stein. That was Tom's idea."

When the group would go on the road, they'd "use an old red school bus and tour to places like Green Bay and Fargo in the midst of winter. It was quite an adventure. Joe Daly would go with us as our driver and Stage Manager," said Susan Chreitzberg (Professor Emeritus at the University of Memphis). About the bus, Tom Leabhart adds, "Well, I don't know if they bought it especially for the occasion, but we had a tour of the South. We toured for six or seven weeks through places like Alabama and Mississippi—all on the bus. We'd sometimes even sleep on the bus. Joey was the bus driver on that tour, with Susan Chrietzberg, Robert Sucher, maybe Val Dean, Karen Flaherty for sure, maybe Joe Long. Yeah, there was a big group all on the bus. I think there must have been a couple of places to lie down on the bus. I don't think everybody could sleep at the same time. I think we slept in shifts."

A review in the Wisconsin State Journal from that time period remarks that the performance titled *Mimeworks* was "designed as a showcase for various styles and techniques in the art of mime developed over the past several decades. Two solo pieces, 'The

Carpenter' and 'The Washerwoman' are highly stylized portraits of the noble spirit of work created by Etienne Decroux. The mime company applied mimetic stylization and movement in two spoken pieces—one, a macabre and zany bedtime story by Gertrude Stein, and the other a work which explores the injustice of sex—role stereotyping in children called 'William s Doll.'"

Talking about the company at this point in time, Leabhart recalls, "I remember enjoying the work. I enjoy working with good heart. I think we created work from all starting points. I think it was sometimes that different people would bring an idea to the company. I can remember that Robert Sucher made a very long clown piece with Karen Flaherty which I looked at more than a couple of times, and made suggestions. At certain moments it was more like a collective. I think that is a good way to describe it. I think other pieces, for example *The Three Sisters Who Are Not Sisters* was done through improvisation. I selected certain moments and we tried to keep those and added on different things. I think improvisation was always the basis for the creation."

Karen Flaherty remembers, "As a company member your life was segmented. It did depend on what style you were practicing. So Doobie (Kay Doobie Potter) and John (Aden) would often do their own rehearsals and creative work. I would often work with James Van Eman and Meg (Partridge) on things. I eventually did learn 'Table, Chair & Glass,' a Tom Leabhart piece. I learned some from Meg, and some from watching Tom teach class. As company members it was expected of us to create pieces and get booked and get out on the road. Tom directed *Three Sisters Who Are Not Sisters*. He saw that as being the centerpiece of other things that would then work around it. He also would perform 'Table, Chair & Glass,' and 'Washerwoman' and 'Carpenter.'"

When Leabhart left the Valley Studio in 1978 to become a Resident Artist at Grand Valley State Colleges in Allendale, MI, many company members went with him or moved on to other projects. The mime company was again fundamentally changed. As the Studio closed in 1979, company members included Dennis

Richards, and others. It must be noted that in addition to the Wisconsin Mime Theatre, there were other performing programs offered by company members and teachers at the Valley Studio. Tom Leabhart remembers them in this way, "For example, John and Doobie had a children s show, a school thing, which they had leftover from before I got there. So they were very important in the Madison schools. They performed a lot in the Madison schools. Reid was still doing his solo show. Reid had two or three solo shows. He had his pantomime show. He had something with folk music with David Crosby, the musical director with the symphony. So all of these things were going on." Also, while the Period Dance master teacher William Burdick was on the faculty, he shared performances of his Dances of the Court and Theatre throughout the region.

YEAR-ROUND STUDY
AT THE VALLEY STUDIO

Although the focus of the training at the Valley Studio began with summer workshops, Terry Kerr recalls, "1974 was the first year of Reid's idea to have a year-round program at the Valley Studio that students would be there through the winter." As the program grew, Gilbert and other company members, as well as guest instructors would teach in those winter months.

As well as teaching mime and self mask, Gilbert recalls, "When Tom Leabhart came I thought it would make more sense for him to teach the specific Decroux technique because he'd studied longer and later than I had. So I invented a new course. I just taught what I called natural movement which was really fun for me. I just developed it. I was actually delighted with that discovery." Full time classes would continue to be taught at the Studio through 1978, and into 1979.

Summers at the Valley Studio Summer sessions were where the Valley Studio really made its mark on training in the United States. Barbara Leigh, commenting on early sessions, says, "There were quite a few different classes in the summer. It was really run with specific sessions each hour. We'd get up and there were early morning stretching and yoga sessions—sun salutation kinds of things. Then we'd also wash the floor. Reid, having studied in the East, had this practice of washing the floor. So we'd do that. Then we'd work with these various teachers on all different aspects of Movement Theater. The sessions would usually culminate in a performance by the students."

As early as the summer of 1972, students could study mime and mask with Leigh & Gilbert, music with Karlos Moser, improvisation with Gloria Shapiro, and acting with Joan Graves. "I think the example of the passion of the teachers who came to Valley Studio and the incredible diversity and creativity that they exhibited were all just very inspirational," states Leigh.

In 1974, the summer faculty included Charles Weidman—Modern Dance, Nilimma Devi—Indian Dance, Robin Reed of the Reed Marionettes—Puppetry, Judith Burgess from Stanford—Acting, and Dr. Bella Itkin, artistic director of the Goodman Children's Theater—Acting. That summer several teachers from the International Festival of Mime in LaCrosse, WI, also stopped in to offer workshops and master classes, including Mamako Yoneyama.

At the end of each summer session the students would share their work in workshop productions, or "Sharings." Throughout the summer these Sharings would be supplemented on other weekends by performances of professional performing arts groups. For example the calendar of events for the summer of 1972 included a classic film series as well as the following performances: The Capitol Trio String Concert, Gestures of the Heart—a performance by Reid Gilbert and the Wisconsin Mime Company, Souvenirs of Opera, The Eye of the Beholder—a dramatic collage, and a Showcase of Total Theatre: Opera...Mime...and Drama. The summer series of 1978 included: The Bacchae directed by Jacques Burdick and starring Peter Hoff. The Wisconsin Chamber Orchestra, William Burdick's Dances of the Court & Theatre, The Corporeal Mime Theatre directed by Thomas Leabhart, Lucknow Kathak performed by Lalli, and the experimental Timewheels directed by Richard Cohn. With performances such as these, the Valley Studio was able to attract the support of townspeople and locals from the surrounding area who came to count on the great entertainment offered up by the Studio and its students. Students were attracted to the Valley Studio by the caliber of the instructors as well as the focus on craft that the rural setting enabled. Reid Gilbert begins, "I m not sure how I ever got those teachers, but boy was I ever lucky. I had some fantastic teachers. Someone would tell me about someone else. Mamako Yoneyama, how did I get in touch with her? I don't know. And of course, Carlo... We had people there teaching karate, and then William Burdick teaching Period Dance, and then of course Jacques Burdick was teaching and directing there in 1978."

Remembering his studies there, John Towsen says, "First I went there with Fred Yockers, my clown partner. We went to study with Carlo. He was the draw for us. In later summers I studied other disciplines. Neither Period Dance nor Corporeal Mime was exactly up my clown alley, but I was trying everything. So, me, klutz with no sense of rhythm, I'm studying dance and corporeal mime. You don't have to be good at something for it to expand your sense of yourself and what you can do. Yes there were practical things I learned that I could list, but also it was a self image and sense of limits that it affected. There I was studying with this famous dancer from the Graham Company.

"I was studying new things that I didn't even know existed, but then it was the multiplicity of them that was also kind of staggering, like Joe Martinez doing Stage Combat and doing the Mao Tze Tung warm-up, then William Burdick doing Period Dance. You had your warring schools of mime and pantomime, South Indian dance, your mask makers, your commedia dell arte, your puppeteers. Whatever they had, as a student it was like you went through a door and there was this whole larger world of things."

Ronlin Foreman recalls his summer of 1977 at the Valley Studio, "The fact that there were a lot of things being offered at the Valley Studio was a plus. I did Carlo and Tom Leabhart at the same time, but I didn't recognize Carlo at the time, so I was mostly only there for Tom. I had been really interested in Decroux's work, especially since the Viterbo Festival. I was trying to find myself in that form. So I went to study with Leabhart. I do remember one other class though where we did work with a Commedia scenario. I remember being terrified because I was not a good reader, and I didn't come from an improvisational background, and was given a script for Arlecchino. Ended up with Carlo being complimentary to me about doing whatever it was that I did. I remember being a little stunned. That opened up a door with my engagement with Carlo over the years."

All participants at the Valley Studio, students and teachers alike, realized that they also were meeting like-minded people they would know and come to depend on throughout their career. About this fact, Jacques Burdick (former Head of the Theatre Department at Adelphi University) recalls, "What made the Valley Studio go was not unity. It was that a great many interesting people, who were interested in working in theater, were there available to teach, and you had to get out of them what you needed. And they all knew why they were there. It was a place to work."

"It was a real crossroads of a lot of people in juggling and circus arts and what we called then New Vaudeville," recalls Tom Leabhart. According to John Towsen, "You didn't know it at the time, but while you were at the Valley Studio, you were meeting colleagues: Ronlin Foreman was up the hill with me in the Shantytown in his tent. That was one of the reasons Fred and I started collaborating with him on the first Clown Festival in New York in '83, which led to all kinds of things. You see Ronlin and Fred and I wanted to produce our shows in New York so we got together and were going to run our shows together and then we kept adding shows. Pretty soon we had this huge festival. That came from the Valley Studio."

Karen Flaherty put it this way, "When I left Valley Studio, the two people who helped me were Reid Gilbert and William Burdick. They got me work all the time. I was constantly working throughout the summer. I was out in Colorado. I was in Ohio. I was in Syracuse. I was with William locally in New York City, and at NYU and Julliard where we did the master classes together. Both of them kept me afloat. My finding an inexpensive place to live in New York helped me to create my one-woman show. I debuted that piece at the Syracuse Festival."

WHY IT ENDED

Although the Valley Studio was successfully fulfilling its mission by performing and teaching theater and other performing arts, it came to a close in 1979. Very succinctly, Reid Gilbert states, "Well, it all ended in 1979 when we had to sell the place because we had a $60,000 debt. It was kind of interesting. Each year we earned . . . and this was unheard of . . . we earned 90 percent of our budget. We had about 5 percent in grants, primarily from the Wisconsin Arts Board, and then the 5 percent was our debt. It was that 5 percent that added up. The board was very supportive emotionally, but not very supportive financially. Some of them could have done much more. Then the last year the Wisconsin Arts Board turned us down. I contacted the head of the board and asked why, and he said, 'We heard you were having money problems.' I said, 'Why do you think we are applying? If I don't need the money I'm not going to apply for it.' Well we sold the place to Michael George who started a retreat center for the arts, primarily for musicians."

THE LEGACY OF THE VALLEY STUDIO

The list of students who attended classes and workshops at the Valley Studio reads like a veritable "Who s Who" of Movement Theater today: Valerie Dean, who passed away in November of 2011, of the Coaching & Creative Support Team for Cirque do Soleil; John Towsen, author of the book Clowns; Ronlin Foreman, currently School Director and teacher at the Dell Arte School in Blue Lake, CA; Marguerite Mathews, Co-Artistic Director of Portsmouth, New

Hampshire's Pontine Theatre; Mike Pedretti, who went on to create Movement Theater International and all the mime festivals in the 1980s; corporeal mime Steve Wasson who will be opening his own school in a converted church in Spring Green this summer; Barbara Leigh, the Artistic/Producing Director at the Milwaukee Public Theatre; Terry Kerr, Karen Flaherty, Daniel Stein, and many more notable movement theater professionals today all were students at the Valley Studio at one time or another.

> *"I think the lesson of the place is you go on learning. There was a wonderful diversity of personalities, a diversity of approaches. It was an intense experience where we made friends that we still have to this day. When you go through any kind of intense experience, there's a kind of a bonding that happens. We make a point of staying in touch because we had that kind of unifying experience together. So I think the Valley Studio was like that as well."*
>
> —Tom Leabhart

> *"I believe that the Valley Studio was a major underpinning for the development of the field in this country—there was a sense that what was happening there was not novelty but a manifestation, in that place and time, of a lineage of cultural and aesthetic and embodied Theatrical practice ... a Physical Theatre with all its mystical and metaphysical aspects."*
>
> —Ronlin Foreman

I dedicate this article to William Burdick, with whom I studied and performed Period Dance at the Valley Studio in 1978. He taught me how to work. –Jef Lambdin, February 2012

Winter night at Valley Studio

Dr. Dean Connor's Story

The property included an old farm house with a bunch of run-down buildings, 175 acres of forest and pasture, a small stream and a barn that the farmer (Newton) had put up as a young farmer when he got married.

I was intrigued by the place, the valley location and the beautiful surroundings. I asked the lady about the hill right overlooking the place. She said that was called rattlesnake hill. But she had never been up there. It turned out that rattlesnake hill became our favorite picnicking spot.

The sale price of the 175 acres was $45 an acre. When the local bank approved my mortgage, I was a very happy man.

I became a friend of a local architect, Herbert Fritz, who had been a student of Frank Lloyd Wright, but then had his own studio and his own style. He recommended moving the farmhouse up near the barn, joining them with some form of a veranda and then modernizing them to make a very livable five-bedroom house. Herb drew up the plans and offered his two resident carpenters to do the job.

I consulted with the local county forester and followed his recommendation to plant evergreens on the poor producing clay soil of the farm land. Then Ben Rogner came to help. In the summer of 1968 we staged a big party for the laboratory personnel that lasted all weekend.

Ben eventually started working with Reid Gilbert, a Methodist minister, a mime and a theater man. Reid began using the place to teach mime and eventually it became a mime studio. To house the students, Herb Fritz designed another building in back of the main house as a dormitory, studio and dining room and kitchen. I bought the Kritz school, an abandoned one-room school near by, and we moved it over to the campus for an additional practice studio.

It was all very exciting and quite wonderful.

Addendum:

It *was* quite wonderful and Dean was soon given the name of Dr. Wonderful by the appreciative students and staff.

erg

The schoolhouse-studio

This is a picture of the schoolhouse when it opened in 1911. It was not only the first day of the building, but also the first day of school for Edna Kritz, who is standing on the front row with one hand behind her back. Her mother asked her, "Edna, why do you have your hand behind you?" Her quick answer was, "Because I hadn't finished my apple." This feisty little girl grew up across Rush Creek from the Studio and became a significant friend of mine and the Studio. I have written more about her (Edna Kritz Meudt) in a later chapter.

The barn before it became a studio and costume room

Newton farmhouse

A New Mime Home

E. Reid Gilbert

Returning from India in 1966, I secured the position of Director of Theatre on the Lambuth College faculty in Jackson, Tennessee. It was obvious that the theatre students needed movement training, so I utilized my interest and techniques of mime for the Lambuth Theatre program.

While on a Fulbright assignment to India, I had taught mime to the acting students at the National School of Drama in New Delhi. My Lambuth students and I wrote and performed a mime evening, *Black and White Dixie*, in which the black students put on white make-up and the white students donned black greasepaint.

In the summers of the late '60s my students and I trekked to Spring Green, Wisconsin where I taught children in the Uplands Arts Council programs. Although mime was only a part of the students' study, they responded positively to this silent form of performance.

A particular performance, in one of the public recitals, was performed by a brother/sister duo. The piece, which they dubbed, *A Drag*, showed them walking in place toward each other and dragging on cigarettes, which of course, were invisible. While still walking, they'd puff until they got down to the stub and then in pantomime they'd light another cigarette. During this time, they'd be silently coughing; only slightly at the beginning, but as they approached (inch by inch) toward each other, the coughing became so severe, until they'd nearly doubled over before collapsing completely on the floor.

The audience received the performance enthusiastically, as they were well aware that the performance was a specific message to the students' father.

The performance was obviously effective, as their dad subsequently quit smoking.

The Lambuth College students, who came with me in the summers, gave several mime performances, including one for a Fourth of July celebration for the rudest audience any of us had ever witnessed. I counseled my students that every performer must have at least one Witwen in their performance career, and after that Fourth of July event they'd already had theirs.

In 1969 I took a leave of absence from Lambuth College to stay in Wisconsin after the Uplands Arts Council Summer Program to finish writing the dissertation for my Ph.D. My family and I rented a wonderful old farm house near Plain, Wisconsin, only a few miles from Taliesin.

A friend of mine, Dr. Dean Connors, lived on the Upper Wyoming Valley Road, only three miles from Taliesin. He asked me if I would give mime instructions to his daughter, Susan, and his houseboy, Ben Rogner, assuring me that I could use the studio space in his renovated barn.

After a few weeks of classes, Dr. Connors suggested that Ben and I start performing in local schools and colleges. We would have the total use of his place for rehearsals, as he was moving into Madison, because he had found it too inconvenient to drive into Madison every day for his position as pathologist at St. Mary's Hospital.

Herbert Fritz, a colleague of Frank Lloyd Wright, had designed the house. He actually had redesigned the house, as he used the old house and barn of the former Newman farm. The house, with two small upstairs bedrooms and a first-floor kitchen and living room, was transported up a small incline to be placed over a finished basement and at an oblique angle to the barn. Herbert then designed a large kitchen between the house and barn, leaving a space between the two structures. He then added a bathroom in the upstairs of the house and one on the bottom level of the barn, in which he designed two bedrooms. The upper level was renovated into a wonderful studio space with a freestanding fireplace. To tie the two structures together he designed a generous roof overhang at the level of the bottom floors covering a wide breezeway. The whole place was a wonderful spot to begin creative work of any kind and certainly movement theatre.

Herbert became a close friend, and I often complimented him on his architectural style of *elegant primitivism.* The purpose of this description of these facilities, is that they were the physical setting of a mime school for nine years.

In 1970 Dr. Connors suggested that I use his Wyoming Valley place as a summer studio for some more students. Subsequently, he and I and a few more friends established the Valley Studio and the Wisconsin Mime Theatre and School as a 501(C)3 nonprofit arts organization..

There were only five students at first. I cooked lunch for them everyday, as I felt that in order for students to receive some kind of educational sustenance from an instructor, it would be helpful also to provide physiological nutritional sustenance.

When we headed the next year into a more serious curriculum with students living at the school, Dr. Connors asked me who the cook was going to be. I said, "I don't know yet. I don't even have the teachers lined up."

He replied, "Well the cook is going to be the most important person there." Subsequently, I did discover how picky people can be about their food, almost as though they're afraid that they may starve. This scenario was part of the impetus for planting and cultivating a substantial garden every summer. When the summer students would arrive they'd be assigned one of three tasks: kitchen, landscape or garden.

This was an arrangement which most students seemed to appreciate, even if they'd had no previous experience with gardening. One young girl, while holding a handful of tomato seeds, asked, "How many of these does it take to make a bush?" When I assured her it required only one seed, after planting and tending, to grow a tomato vine, she was astounded.

One summer student objected to the work assignments. She was a public school teacher and was angry, as she had been counting on her study of mime to be a summer holiday. She said, "I didn't pay all this money (the costs were minimal) to come out here and have to work. I suppose you do that in order to keep costs down."

I replied, "I do not include these work assignments to keep costs down, but because I see the total experience – living together, taking classes together, working in this wonderful natural environment and sharing work together – as integral to any educational or creative benefits."

She said, "Well I don't like it."

"I'll be happy to refund your money if you would like to leave."

She left to the great relief of everyone. I have discovered that miserable people are quite generous, as they love to share their misery.

Other students took delight in their work assignments, as it was a break from the classes and often supplied wonderful opportunities for horseplay. The kitchen equipment was as substantial as that of nearby restaurants, but the students gave them pet names, due to their individual personalities, particularly the Hobart dishwasher. Quite often I'd hear that Hobart was sick again and was throwing up all over the kitchen.

During one kitchen cleanup time, two of the students used Hobart's water faucet extension for a water battle and subsequently broke it. Like school children they brought the broken pieces to me, assuring me that they'd pay for the repairs, which, of course, I expected them to do.

The summer students ranged across a wide spectrum of interests and backgrounds. Even the full-time winter students included not only college age students but also a clinical psychologist and a university dean on sabbatical leave.

Early in the '70s, I performed in the Play Circle at the Student Union at the University of Wisconsin. After the performance, a woman and her eight-year-old son talked with me about mime and the son's interest in studying with me. I told her that my school was a residential school and that my students were mostly of college age. They both pursued the matter until I relinquished and told them I would be happy to accept him in the coming summer's enrollment. He attended for four summers, and the older students were happy to include him in the classes as well as in their extracurricular activities, such as swimming in the nearby Wisconsin River.

When I moved to Tucson, I discovered that that young student, Grant Bashore, was an attorney in Tucson. Occasionally nowadays Grant performs a solo mime show.

As the enrollment increased we expanded the facility itself: two small dormitories up the hill from the original buildings and an extension of the farmhouse for an office and an apartment for the director. These additions could then accommodate fifty residential students.

In 1976, we were able to purchase a one-room schoolhouse about a mile away. We moved it to our property, thereby adding another indoor studio space to our other two. For our summer classes we also had two outdoor class/performance spaces.

The *New York Times* declared Valley Studio as "the center of mime training in this country." This was due in large part, not only to the facility and natural environment, but also to the instructors we were able to engage.

William Burdick, who had been Ballet Master of the Metropolitan Opera Ballet, taught Ballet and Period Movement. Carlo Mazzoni Clementi, the founder of Del Arte School of Physical Theatre, taught Commedia Del Arte and Physical Comedy. Mamako Yoneyama, who had studied with Marcel Marceau, taught Zen Mime. Barbara Leigh taught French Theatre. Daystar Rosalie Jones, a Blackfeet Indian, taught Modern Dance and Native American Dance. Karlos Moser, Director of Opera at the University of Wisconsin, taught Opera Workshops. David Crosby, Director of the Wisconsin Chamber, toured with us as an acompanist and taught choral music. I taught Mime and Acting. James Roose-Evans, the West End director chosen by Tennessee Williams to direct his London scripts, taught Improvisational Theatre. Indian dance was taught by Gina Lalli (Kathak) and Nillimma Devi (Bharat Natyam). Avner, The Eccentric, taught clown.

One of the mime company members, Joe Daly, pursued his interest in *Bharata Natyam* by studying the dance form in India for several years. He became one of the best *Bharata Natyam* teachers in New York City.

Another popular instructor was Hovey Burgess, a faculty member of NYU. He taught circus techniques, including juggling, balancing and trapeze. The summer that he brought his trapeze, we had to find a truck to reach a limb on a white oak tree in the front yard to attach the trapeze. Even today, Hovey enjoys telling how we got the trapeze down. When it was time to take the trapeze down, the truck was not there, so I said, "I'll get it down." I then took my shoes off and shinnied up the tree. I chided Hovey by reminding him that, "You're the trapeze artist. I'm just an old 'possum hunter."

In 1977, Thomas Leabhart left his position on the faculty of the University of Arkansas and joined our faculty and staff full-time, bringing along with him several of his own students. This enlarged our traveling troupe considerably. Tom then taught Corporeal Mime, as he had studied with Decroux for a longer time than I had. I then taught the Fundamentals of Movement – almost a history of movement from that of an amorphous amoeba to crawling then walking and ultimately to use hand tools, both singly and shared. I had tried to teach cross-cut saw to people before, but not very satisfactorily. However, when we progressed to the shared tools, the students immediately learned the appropriate technique and surprised me by cutting quickly through a large hardwood tree that had fallen across a woods lane. They had been able to take their earlier work in rudimentary movement, including rhythm and balance to the task of using a crosscut saw.

During the regular school terms we'd perform primarily in

the Wisconsin area, but also had extended tours all the way from North Dakota to Georgia.

Various adjunct instructors led short-term classes and workshops in many other disciplines. Herbert Fritz, our architect, often led seminars on architecture and particularly the architecture of Frank Lloyd Wright. Others led workshops in music, photography and karate.

One of our board members, Edna Meudt, was a nationally-recognized poet and would often share with us some of her poetry. She was born just across the creek from the studio. An interesting bit of trivia: Edna had attended the schoolhouse which we'd moved, and she gave us a picture of the schoolhouse, taken the first day it was used and also of the students, standing in front of it. It was also Edna's first day of school. She was the smallest pupil in the picture.

Edna also wrote a three-act play on the life and times of Governor Dodge, which our theatre company produced – with words – at the old theatre in Mineral Point.

One Saturday afternoon a tornado hit Edna's farm, south of Dodgeville, ten miles away. She called to say she'd have to cancel the visit she had planned for Valley Studio that evening. Her barn had been blown off its foundation and several of her trees were down. The next morning I took nearly all of the summer students to help Edna clean up. Her favorite tree, a large larch, had been completely uprooted, and she had already called someone with a crane to come on Monday to place it upright again.

One of the students, Cleatius Gouldman, looked at the exposed roots of the larch and asked Edna if she had any old clean sheets, which he could cut up. She brought such a sheet, and he ripped it into two-inch wide strips, about two feet long and tied them like ribbons on many of the roots. Then he put another wet sheet over the whole rootball. Edna, who was a wise farm woman herself, said, "Why did you do that?"

Cleatius, whose heritage was Blackfeet Indian, said, "So that the tree spirit will know we haven't forgotten it." The tree was set

upright by a crane the following Monday and has now outlived
Edna by several decades.

The summer terms were divided into two-week long sessions,
with some students enrolling for all of the sessions. Each session
would culminate with the classes presenting a performances of
their work. The mime performances, of course, were always filled
with delight. William Burdick's Period Dance classes were vivacious
and colorful with authentic costumes., which William would always
bring with him each year. The outdoor stage was at the foot of a
slope directly across from the slope with the dormitories. At the
end of one of Mamako's classes, her students lined themselves
across the ridges of the three visible buildings and performed a
stunning choreographed ritualistic dance.

As exotic as some of this movement study and performances
were, it was also important to us to be as involved in the local
community as much as possible. We always welcomed local folks
to our presentations and special events.

Several times during the summer, David Crosby would bring
the Wisconsin Chamber Orchestra out to Valley Studio to perform
on the front porch of the house. Our guests often included the
staff and apprentices at Taliesin. The audience sat on the gentle
grassy slope of the front yard. Quite often, as the orchestra would
be finishing the concert, the whip-o-wills would begin their evening
song, seemingly in tune and rhythm with the human musicians.
One such performance, *Appalachia andOther Folk,* was filmed as a
PBS Special.

The large front yard was also utilized for other activities,
ranging from outdoor classes and play, including an occasional
wedding. Some of the students and staff, including some neighbor
couples, would take advantage of my ecclesiastical credentials and
ask me to officiate at their weddings in the front yard. During one
such wedding, it was raining fiercely, and, as I was wearing my
academic regalia I pulled the doctoral hood over my head to protect
my head from the downpour. One of the gathered celebrants stated,

"That's the first time I've ever seen anyone really use their PhD hood in such a practical manner."

We began in the mid-seventies to extend our interests in the mime world to festivals, Washington performances and the International Mimes and Pantomimists.In 1974 we cooperated with Viterbo College in LaCrosse, Wisconsin, with an international mime festival in which our whole mime company had a chance to meet and interact with various styles and headliners from around the globe.

An interesting event happened in the final week of the festival in August. Broadcasts were filled with news that President Nixon was going to make an important announcement. All festival activities stopped while everyone watched Nixon's resignation speech. It was a somber time for the Americans as well as the international attendees. However one of the participants, Fialka, seemed to be ecstatic. I said to him, "I don't understand your attitude. This is a sad day for all Americans, both those who were Nixon's supporters as well as his adversaries."

Fialka countered my dismay by saying, "I'm an American now."

I said, "I know that."

He said, "If this kind of political shenanigans had happened in most any other country in the world, either the leader would be assassinated or he would have wiped out his political enemies. Today we're reminded that there is a country that can heal its own political wounds, and I'm now a naturalized citizen of that country, and I'm celebrating."

This lesson that we all needed to hear was delivered, quite appropriately at an international mime festival – the wordless art form that doesn't recognize national or cultural boundaries.

In 1975 I was asked to lead the International Mimes and Pantomimists (IMP) which had been founded five years earlier by Paul Curtis in New York City. Valley Studio and the Wisconsin Mime Theatre and School became the headquarters of IMP for five years. We kept in touch with regional representatives around the world, primarily with *The Mime News* a bi-monthly newspaper of reviews, opinion and announcements. Thomas Leabhart, the Artisitc Director of the Wisconsin Mime Theatre and School, was the editor. As the Administrator of IMP, I had the opportunity to write the Administrators Column, which I placed right on the front page.

The most significant column was the one in which I upbraided so many of the critics who had begun, in their critiques and reviews, to imply an orthodoxy of a specific mime style. The issue of a deadly orthodoxy in any endeavor, remains a crucial issue, thus a few excerpts from that column in the March/April 1979 issue:

> For some strange reason or reasons these diatribes (reviews)have been aimed at any mimes who are reminiscent of Marcel Marceau.... If the "well worn 'white-faced Marcel Marceau' style" is unacceptable, can we no longer use the red clown nose which is also "well worn"? It is strange indeed to read pious accolades of "inspired by Buster Keaton" or "created by Etienne Decroux" by the same writers who denigrate any influences by Marceau as "copies". There is no quarrel that a superficial copy of a style or technique should be exposed as such, whether it is from Robert Shields's robot, Etienne Decroux's triple design or Marceau's fluttering butterfly, but to imply that no one can create illusion walls anymore because Marceau has done them is to prevent Baryshnikov from dancing any roles performed by Nijinsky and to preclude any more Hamlets because it has already been done. ... Great concern has been expressed that there seems to be developing a sentiment for "correct" styles and "incorrect" styles, an attitude which borders on fascism. ... (in Japan) The Noh uses masks, Kabuki uses stylized makeup. The Japanese culture embraces both of these styles. ... (To quote Marceau) "The Russian Theatre uses the Marceau style, the circus style, acrobatic style, and dance style; and they make a combination of pantomime which belongs to them, but they reject nobody. I think that rejection is a part of frustrated love and immaturity."

As Administrator of IMP, I was invited to speak – not mime – at an all-Canada Mime Festival. It was a gala affair with more than two hundred attendees. However, my spoken address was successfully upstaged by a fellow in a tuxedo, who kept pretending a limp as he crossed several times right in front of the speaker's lectern. I suppose it was a little incongruous to have someone give an oration at a mime festival.

In 1978 I co-directed the Festival of American Mime at the Milwaukee Performing Arts Center and was successful in having Joan Mondale represent the Carter Administration to draw attention to the increasingly popular art of mime. I had already performed, solo, at Vice-President Mondale's official residence in Washington and also at the Senate Finance Committee Dinner Party.

It was at the dinner party that after my silent performance and bow, I announced, "Mimes can talk, and I urge all of you in this august assemblage to support the arts, whether mime or opera." That night I met several cabinet members and senators, including Senator Dole and Senator Robert Byrd. Years later, Senator Byrd became my senator when I moved to West Virginia.

Back to the Milwaukee festival: I had booked Jacques Lecoq of Paris to deliver the keynote address – *Toute Bouges* (Everything Moves). It was a brilliant presentation, for which I thanked him and paid him. A couple of months after the festival I received a letter from Lecoq's agent, stating that I owed his client more money. Angrily, I replied that M. Lecoq had addressed the festival for which he was amply paid according to our contract, and I had no intention to pay any extra assessment and was insulted by the request. The agent answered by saying that Lecoq would not insist on more money but that I needed to understand that he had not only spoken those words, but that he had also written them and he could rightfully claim an author's royalty.

E. REID GILBERT

I must now let the participants (students, instructors, staff) tell their stories.

Period Dancers on the lawn

Encountering the Art of Mime

Craig McIntosh

As a fifteen-year-old in 1967, I first encountered Reid Gilbert and the art of mime at a University of Wisconsin, Madison high school drama camp, where Reid presented a mime workshop. I was immediately enthralled by this unfamiliar art form that combined my lifelong athleticism with a theatrical means of communication delivered in complete silence. Starting the following year, I spent three of the next four summers at the Valley Studio. In 1968, I began my intensive mime training with Reid, and performed in my first mime show, as a member of the Uplands Players. The following year, I was a member of the newly-formed Uplands Repertory Theatre, continuing my mime training under Reid, and performing in all four productions, in repertory: a mime show, a dance program, a drama, and a musical. In 1970, at the suggestion of Reid, because he knew of a mime on the faculty there (Reid wasn't going to be teaching college that year), I began my undergraduate studies in Theatre at Lewis & Clark College, in Portland, Oregon, where I studied under Franz Reynders, and performed with the Oregon Mime Company.

In the summer of 1971, I returned to the Valley Studio to be a member of the nascent Wisconsin Mime Theatre, touring around the state, performing on street corners and in schools. One high school provided a unique challenge to our performance. At intermission, I used the downstairs restroom, only to discover, upon attempting to exit, that I was locked in. The doorknob simply did not work. After several sequential apologies for the delay to the audience, by

31

Reid, for the delay and a broken pair of scissors, bested by industrial strength of the recalcitrant doorknob, I was warned to stand aside. After several very loud banging noises, the door knob flew across the bathroom, the door opened, and I was greeted heartily by the three-piece-suited school superintendent, with a hammer in his hand and a huge grin on his face, who seemed to have greatly enjoyed freeing a mime trapped in an actual box and (I always thought) took a curious delight in beating the crap out of a school door, in a sort of "man-over-machine" moment. This was not the only lesson I learned that summer, but it certainly taught me to test every unfamiliar doorknob before locking, whenever I toured a show of any kind – a "safety check" I practice to this very day. You just never know where the important lessons will come from.

I treasure those years in Spring Green. In each of those summers, I lived with the Gilbert family, becoming the "summer brother" to Reid's three wonderful young daughters. I learned about Etienne Decroux and Marcel Marceau and Jack Tales and No theatre and Kathakali dance and Frank Lloyd Wright. I worked with wonderfully gifted artists – talented locals and folks who, like myself, came from afar to spend their summers learning from, and working, with Reid, a true Renaissance man. After – and because of – those summers in Spring Green, I graduated from Lewis & Clark College and earned an MFA in Drama from the University of California, Irvine. I have performed in various theatre companies throughout the western United States. The mime training from Reid laid the groundwork for more than 40 years of performing mime, from Anchorage, Alaska to Edinburgh, Scotland, Southern California to Chicago, Illinois, and many, many points in between. I performed solo shows and worked in Artist-in-Education programs, doing mime and improvisational theatre. I've guest-directed plays and musicals at various universities and schools, and, now, I am the sole theatre faculty and artistic director at a community college in rural eastern Oregon, where, every winter term, I include a mime component in my acting class, and carry on the legacy of Reid Gilbert and the Valley Studio for yet another generation.

B. H. Barry and Don Rieder, Mutual Support

Moon Landing

J. Lynn West

Situating a theatre between two bars may be appropriate but is asking for trouble with the actors. As I remember, during the summer of '69 the actors had to actually walk (or run) through the bar (the name of which I don't remember) behind the stage to make some entrances. Occasionally there was enough time for a quick drink. One night John Juhl apparently availed himself of a libation, or more than one, before the show. At one point the statement was made that the forest rangers were marching into "death and possible danger." Also, John didn't manage to get his pants zipped up and onstage he told Monona (Little Mary) that "a forested ranger is truly a man" and she looked pointedly crotchward as she replied "Yes, Captain Big Jim, he is."

Also that summer, attendance was sometimes low and I believe one night we did a performance for three people. We asked them to move down front and gave then a worthy performance (I don't remember which show it was, though; probably not the one in which fellow cast members took delight in nearly drowning Dan Curry – who took acting very seriously – during his baptism in the tub).

MISCELLANEOUS MEMORIES OF THE FARMHOUSE

It was a magnet for eccentrics, ne'er-do-wells and hippies both bona fide and plastic (I fell more into the polyurethane range).

The Chinese troupe who spoke no English. Dean Connors solemnly telling everyone his pathology experience confirmed that ice cream softens the brain. My good friends Shella and Thistle (the dogs). Listening to the sound of snow at night (which I marveled at; we never have enough snow here in Mississippi to make noise, and if we did there would not be the solitude of Upper Wyoming Valley).

Almost every year there was some sort of gardening effort across the road. For whatever reason, the only crop I can remember as being successful was squash – seemingly all manner of squash but mostly acorn and maybe yellow crookneck. Slathering it with butter and cooking it in 37 different ways failed to conceal the fact it was still squash. To this day I will flee from a squash unless it has been boiled to near obliteration and paired with some turnip greens. The food was not that bad but every once in a while I quietly slipped into town and asked the lady at the Dutch Kitchen (I think I remember her name but not how to spell it) to prepare me a good steak and baked potato. Another town treat was the A&W with the frosted root beer mugs and excellent burgers and fries. And then there was the Corner Bar, later Bob's House of Friends. Cokes (or pops, I believe) were 50 cents and tap beer was 15 cents a glass, later increased to 20 cents. I should have died many times over as the result of a friendly night at Bob's House and 15-cent beer.

The diversity of students at Valley Studio was considerable. We had hippies, lesbians, true actors, farm girls, squeakey-clean all-Americans – nearly everything. One summer one of the students was named Courtney Marvin and this was the year "All in the Family" debuted on TV. There was a raging discussion as to whether the show helped support or oppose racial intolerance and she ended the discussion by assuring everyone Carroll O'Connor would not be a part of it if it fostered intolerance. That's because, she said, she knew him personally. As far as I know, no one ever questioned how it was that she knew an actor who had had a major role in "Cleopatra" with Elizabeth Taylor and Richard Burton. Only at the end of the summer was it revealed she was the daughter of actor, Lee Marvin.

Early one spring a rattlesnake kept trying to get in the barn part of the house, probably not fully having its wits about it, and I killed it. For some reason Heather Wallace decided she wanted to tan the snake skin and make it into a belt. She unleashed her Swiss Army Knife, read up some, got some salt and worked assiduously on the skin for what seemed like weeks. Despite her best efforts the snakeskin ended up looking worse than roadkill.

During the early years the Wisconsin Mime Company was fighting a turf war (actually for street space rather than turf) directly or indirectly with the Kentucky Fried Theatre from the Madison area. It may not have been that big a deal but the Kentucky Fried Theatre members, Jim Abrahams and brothers David and Jerry Zucker, went on to successful film careers ("Kentucky Fried Movie," "Airplane," "Police Squad," "Top Secret!" "Hot Shots," "Scary Movie," "Mafia"and "The Naked Gun" among others). In not all, but in many of their movies violence is done to a Mime sometime during the action. Did the Wisconsin Mime Company cause this?

FROM THE FIRST SUMMER

Somewhere, nearly 45 years later, I still have clothes with brown stains. The cause might not be an obvious one, however. In "Little Mary Sunshine" I not only stage-managed but played the aged guide Fleetfoot. I wore very little so much makeup was needed and the medium used was a product called "Texas Dirt." It apparently really was Texas dirt and one night a week I was covered in it. About that time my glasses broke so I spent some time half-naked, covered in dirt and running around in the dark wearing sunglasses. Despite long showers after each show my clothes still exhibited strange brown stains for years.

We lived something of an isolated life with little exposure to outside news or TV in Upper Wyoming Valley, which was not bad. We did spend the summer of '69 unaware of something called Woodstock and Hurricane Camille (when I returned home at the end of the summer I found that Camille had taken out the two giant trees in our yard – and we lived more than 300 miles from the Gulf Coast) but did not miss Apollo 11's moon landing. Life was generally very good, although I never developed a taste for brats, fondue or pasties, and could never find anything even remotely resembling barbecue.

Perhaps the reason I don't remember more is because I was there long enough to become something of a local – maybe more a resident of Spring Green than the Valley Nation. I don't know, but it was a memorable time, influential in many ways both good and bad. A lot was accomplished, mostly on a shoestring budget.

When I returned to New Albany I began working at the local newspaper on a temporary basis, just for something to do and help them out. I stayed about 25 years, eventually becoming editor after holding various positions and being a columnist. The newspaper had been purchased by a national chain in the late 1970s and general managers did not last more than a couple of years before moving on. The last one during my tenure appeared to be psychotic, randomly promoting, demoting and firing people. He removed all the doors in the building so he could sneak up on employees and had a voice stress analyzer in his desk because he assumed people were lying to him all the time. He also kept a record of "tells" he believed people exhibited when they were lying to him.

I got to the point when it was too taxing to go to work any more and retired (the man was later found to have a brain tumor, which may or may not have contributed to his behavior).

When I retired, the general manager in question had drastically hurt the image of the newspaper so circulation, advertising and community support were way down.

A few months later in 2006 I and a couple of other newspaper people started our own newspaper, which I proudly note was pretty gutsy in a small community, but we knew we had support before starting.

Our intent was to be primarily a web-based news outlet primarily supported by a print product, based on the premise that everyone was turning to the internet for news. As it turned out, people still wanted the printed version more and not nearly everyone in our area had even decent internet service anyway.

Still, we turned a small profit the first year and about 18 months in received a purchase offer from the Tupelo paper, which owned several other area publications. Part of the sale deal was that I stayed with the paper because I was the franchise, as I had been at the Gazette. This was mostly that I had been around for so long people were comfortable with me and I had a good reputation for accuracy and fairness.

Finally, about two years ago, the Tupelo paper also purchased the New Albany Gazette, the long-time local paper I had left. At that point they discontinued the paper we started and I went back to the Gazette as editor. I now work in the same office as 10 years ago. People still say they miss the paper we had but I am being able to move some of the best parts of our paper into the old Gazette.

I have been married 29 years to a former on-air radio personality and music director who was one of the best in the state. About seven years ago she suddenly began exhibiting signs of one of the forms of schizophrenia and though medication has helped some, life has been a challenge for us, dealing with the paranoia, delusions and hallucinations. Partly because of the medication her weight has more than doubled and she has developed secondary physical problems, too. She was unable to have children because of childhood abuse, which was a disappointment but perhaps for the best considering her illness.

I told you about the appendix surprise before Christmas, which they said I was lucky to have survived. I continue to regain strength.

My obituary will say I was a member of the Rotary Club, president of the Historic Northside Neighborhood Association, president of the Northeast Mississippi Amateur Radio Club, served on the Union County E-911 Commission, served on the New Albany Tourism Advisory Board and was chairman of the Administrative Board of Trustees of the Union County Library System.

In other words, I appear to be well-suited for conservative, unimaginative small-town life in many ways.

It will not say I was one of the blessedly attractive New Albany males who inherited quite a bit of money and did not have to struggle for success (one of the reasons I eventually left the Rotarians).

I also was one of the founders of the Tallahatchie River Players and am a member of the Tallahatchie Arts Council but because newspaper work requires 60-plus hours of work a week, I am not able to give either one much practical support. Perhaps if and when I retire, I can but I don't think I can afford to retire even though it's getting tougher with age 70 coming up this summer.

For years, I have had mixed feelings about returning to Spring Green, somewhat afraid that the reality would ruin the memory. I have done the Google Earth street view of the village, however.

For a long time, Spring Green has held a hallowed, almost mythical, place in my mind.

As years pass, that sense has faded some.

I have a lot of weird dreams due to medication and many of them are repetitive but I never dream about Wisconsin for some reason. I wonder why that is and what it may mean.

Still, taking the bad with the good, those were some of the best few years of my life.

I honestly don't remember, but I think we got to see some of the moon landing on the TV at the Corner Bar, and it was David Pyron who came up with the idea of stapling the small American flag on the ascending moon in "Little Mary Sunshine."

Addendum

The moonlanding to which Lynn was alluding happened in the summer of 1969 when Stanley Godfrey directed "Little Mary Sunshine" at the Gard Theatre. When the song, "The Moon Comes Over the Mountain", a bright orange cardboard moon arose from behind the mountain scenery. On the day the astronauts landed on the moon was the same day as one of the performances, and at which time when the moon began to rise the audience was thrilled to see a little American flag waving from our ersatz moon. Lynn claims that David Pyron contributed the moon.

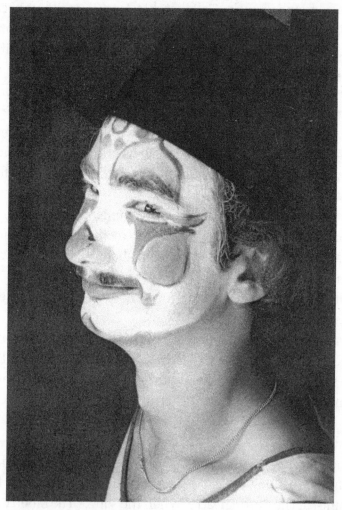

David Harper, A Lovable Clown

The Uplands – Summer 1967

Pamela Stefansson

Saturday night in Spring Green – quiet weekend planned with my grandfather.

Art Baryenbruch has tickets for the opening of the Gard Theatre; do we (my mother and I) want them? Sure! We went. I was hooked.

Weekends throughout the summer, when I wasn't working (waitressing at Hoffman House at the Airport in Madison), out to SG we'd drive, see the performance and then head for the Rathskeller in the Uplands Barn for beer, summer sausage & cheese and music. Kent was bartending; he and Annie and Rick would sing – as would Ron and whoever else was around. Friday nights: silent movies! Room packed with people – director chairs, benches, long tables. Everyone was a friend.

August nights: clear skies, sky full of stars, cool air and ground fog in the valley. On full moon nights: surreal, magical, another world.

The Treehouse Gift Shop – Derry's shop was addictive; I still have the dress made of the Indian bedspread I bought there. Sadly the mice ate all my seed necklaces.

The workshops: because I was slaving in Madison, couldn't attend but wanted to!

THE GARD THEATRE – 1968

Heralded the end of my college career; blew off an English Lit exam at the University of Cincinnati to get up to SG in time to take the Lee Strasberg Workshop that June. Spent the summer in

SG, became a volunteer usherette at the Gard – for almost every performance. Supervised by Archie Sarrazin – learned more from watching those shows than any acting class to date. 'Names': Michael Fairman, Charles Kimborough, Marc Alaimo, Michael Tucker – all wonderful and hilarious. Also: Penelope Reed and Erica Slezak – the diva to end all.

One memory: schlepping Jeremy Fairman around the block, getting him to sleep so his babysitter (Linelle Steele) could take a breather. 'We' enjoyed sniffing the petunias outside the Dutch Kitchen and MaryAnn didn't mind at all when 'we' would pick one to take upstairs (to the Fairman abode above the Corner Bar).

THE GARD THEATRE – 1969

Secretary of the Uplands Arts Council + Gard box office manager. Not particularly gifted at either but had fun. Little Mary Sunshine! Ron Baker. Lynn West. David Pyron – still in touch with Lynn and David.

VALLEY STUDIO –
FALL 1972 – SPRING 1973

Back to waitressing (the Karakahl this time) on weekends; classes all week and prepping for workshops on weekends. Lived in the 'fireplace room' across from the room housing Nancy Quarton (my cousin), Julie, Terry Finman and Heather. Lynn was upstairs in the house. Shared meals in the kitchen. Big breakfasts up in the dorm on weekends – Carie Graves cooking. Making our own yogurt and granola.

The night the earthquake hit. All but Lynn were in the kitchen. We all just sat there, watching the cupboard doors open & close. Then: silence. Lynn flew down the steep stairs and blew into the kitchen. 'WHAT WAS THAT?' to which we all looked at each other blankly and said

'WHAT?'

Classes, classes, classes. Performing at schools all spring. Biggest crowd: 4,000 in Milwaukee. Awesome!

Moral of the story: the Uplands and Valley Studio gave me what I'd needed when I needed it: a window onto the world of the arts, and a doorway to cross through into that world. I've never looked back or regretted one moment of it.

How I First Heard About Valley Studio

Nancy Quarton-Harakay

I first heard about Valley Studio from my cousin Pamela Stefansson. I signed up for the first summer (19?). I enjoyed the multifaceted performing arts experience so much that I approached Reid about offering an apprenticeship program. That fall Terry Finman, Beth (?), Heather (?) and I pioneered the 'first year round' Valley Studio apprentice program.

Other than attending diverse performing arts classes (Mime, Puppetry, Kabuki, Opera, Acting etc.) under the tutelage of skilled instructors worldwide, some of my favorite memories are:

Six AM yoga class conducted on raked pea gravel. Carrie Graves's meals, The Cellar on Bill T's farm, Carlo's morning song & tempura daylilies. Guest Japanese mime Mamako & Chinese Shadow puppetry.

My assessment of the total Valley Studio experience.

What of my experience there I have been able to use since then, including current activity or thoughts.:

The theatre practices I learned at Valley Studio have led me to many extraordinary experiences. I worked with Tennessee Williams (who saw me performing street mime and asked me to help with their production of Animal Farm, Summer & Smoke and Night Of The Iguana) in Key West at his Green Street Theatre in the early 70s. Wherever I traveled – theatre seemed to pursue me because of my unique training at Valley Studio. I ended up in Ketchum, Idaho where I have taught children's theatre & workshops for more than 40 years.

Nina Edming, Business Manager, Mother Confessor,
Intermediary

I Loved This Job

Carie Graves

I spent the summer of 1972 at Valley Studio as the cook for the new mime school. I had just finished my freshman year of college at the University of Wisconsin and needed a job. Reid knew my family. My brother and I had participated in one of his Mime camps several years before as 11 and 12 year olds. I would have loved to have participated in the 72' school but finances prevailed and I needed a job so I was in the kitchen cooking for about 20 teachers and students for lunch and dinner up in the renovated barn.

I loved this job. I LOVED THIS JOB! I always had liked to cook most likely because I always had loved to eat. We had 5 children in our family and we were all big eaters and big kids. Needless to say, there were seldom leftovers after we sat down to eat at our house.

In my eyes that kitchen was state of the art. There was a huge new gas range, a large new bread maker with a dough hook, a big walk-in pantry and a side by side state of the art refrigerator/ freezer. Everything in the kitchen was new and shiny. The best part was that I did not have to do any shopping. Every 3 days or so I wrote a grocery list, gave to one of the interns, who in turn took it up to Dodgeville and went shopping for me.

My favorite part was obsessing over the menus. I studied cook-books and recipes in the evenings.

I've done a lot since then, been a rowing coach for the past 36 years, now retired. Been on 3 Olympic teams etc. etc. But that job at Valley Studio, that was special for me. It made me feel confident. It made me feel I could do anything.

Dear Fellow Studioites

Barbara Leigh

It is a treat to be able to share with you memories of such a formative time and place in my life. My first introduction to any aspect of the Studio was when I was a grad student of Theatre at UW Madison in 1971 (I think...). I was walking on State Street past People's (Paul's?) Bookstore and saw a poster for a Mime show to be performed in a nearby church. I had never seen mime before, and I was particularly interested, since I was working on a dissertation about an acting school in France (L'Ecole du Vieux Colombier) that incorporated mime as basic to actor training.

I was completely enchanted by the performance. Amazing! One person could become multiple characters, rocks, trees, flowers, the wind—everything!! Of course I was eager to talk with the performer to find out more about the art form. And of course the performer was E. Reid Gilbert. Amazingly, Reid had studied with Etienne Decroux, the "Father" of modern mime—and had been one of the students of the Vieux Colombier School!!

AND Reid was about to start workshops in Mime. Well I thought the best way for me to understand what I was writing about was to experience it, so I quickly enrolled in the classes. And that summer Reid was offering more extensive training at Valley Studio—so I jumped at the opportunity to immerse myself in the art. And when I saw the Studio itself, so stunning, and in such a lush, beautiful-if-hot-and-mosquitoey environment, I did not want to leave.

Around the same time, I was planning to go to France to work on my dissertation and run a theatre workshop in London—so I could experience more of the types of activities that were taught in the V.C. School. (There were very few actual theatre courses taught at UW at the time.) It was a hugely creative time for me, and the opportunities to meet and work with such creative people in London, France and Valley Studio gave me a grounding that has been with me ever since.

I have wonderful memories of jogging at night in Wyoming Valley on country roads bathed in moonlight, swimming in the Wisconsin River, sweltering from exercise and sun in the barn studio, watching everyone else dripping in the wall-to-wall mirrors; in the Winter, hunkering around the wood stove, slogging through massive snow drifts, marveling at the icicles that made the Studio into an Ice Palace. And performing an old English play at Folklore Village during Christmas/New Years, surrounded by enthusiastic dancers, folk singers, musicians, crafts artists, the great hall scented in pine from trees decorated in holiday traditions, dancing round dances, square dances, snake dances until the wee hours. And watching spectacular storms from the Uplands Studio, fiery lightning flashes thundering through the valley, shaking the frail barn.

I found a few notes from the period of some of the shows we were working on at Valley Studio. In August of 1971 we did a show called "Bits and Pieces" with a small troupe in a small theatre in Spring Green: Laura Shepperd, Craig McIntosh, Lynn West, Reid and myself. It opened with "Feet" (only seen under a curtain, expressing different characterizations); short sketches, a Japanese Noh piece (River Crossing?), a Vaudeville piece, a poem (Round River Canticle by Edna Meudt) and commedia. Other short pieces we worked on during that period whose names I wrote down are: The Cat and the Pigeon, Cotton Candy, Midnight Snack, The Flag, The Soldier, Suicide, Underwater, Rain Dance, Mad Scientist, Evolution, Butterfly, Flowers, Jack in the Box. I remember also doing a very fun piece, full of slides and falls, called "Skating". We also did "Spider and Fly".

I also have Reid's Outline of Mime Sessions: Exercises and Principles—in case anyone would like a copy. And lots of notes on various exercises. I remember working with Mamako, from Japan, and seeing her perform an intense piece wearing a gas mask. And the amazing mimes from around the world that came to the Studio and/or to the International Mime Festival, held later in Milwaukee, 1978.

The Studio had difficulty maintaining a year-round schedule, so in the Winter we toured the State in 1971/2??, going to various colleges, schools, universities, churches. I remember noisy auditoriums full of children who practically held their breath when we silently came onstage. That always felt like a miracle...(!) That you didn't have to talk to get people's attention.

I moved back to Milwaukee in 1973, and taught a Mime and Improv class there, where I met Mike Moynihan and Terri Kerr. In 1974 Mike and I founded "Friends Mime Theatre", and we continued to take part in workshops at Valley Studio. It was expanding during that period, with a beautiful new dormitory on the hill which also housed a large kitchen. A small studio that was formerly a one-room school-house was also brought onto the property. I remember the smell and feel of the ancient wooden floor, the breeze through the old windows.

I also remember working with Carlo Mazzone-Clementi on Commedia, his energy and dynamic instructions—and myself performing as "Dottore" in our finale summer performance. I had just finished my dissertation and deliriously burned some of my endless notes as part of the play. Whee!

I have continued to work in the theatre ever since—creating original theatreworks with their roots in movement and visual theatre, incorporating music, puppetry, circus, dance...Our company changed its name to Milwaukee Public Theatre in 1991. We are an Outreach company that also has a major educational and healing arts focus—providing workshops and arts residencies in all art forms for people of all ages.

I was severely injured in an accident in December of 1987 and am partially paralyzed. A big part of my healing was the creation of an original one-woman show, "The Survival Revival Revue".

It's a comedy (sometimes dark...) incorporating mime, music and puppetry. Long story short, Mike left the company in '94, so I took over as Artistic/Producing Director—a job I am continuing to do.

Our plans for 2011 include touring two new shows, FLOW, THE TRAVELING WATER CIRCUS, (about water—for children, youth and families) and FROM THE START CONSIDER THE FINISH—for adults, about end of life care and hospices. We'll also continue to tour several other shows that are in our repertoire and to offer workshops/residencies and a major public art project, the All-City People's Parade—inspired by the May Day celebration by In the Heart of the Beast Puppet and Mask Theatre.

We would love to hear from any other artists from the Studio! You can check out our website at www.milwaukeepublictheatre. org. And/or call us at 414-347-1685.

Thanks to Reid for pulling us together again!

Edna Meudt, "A Literary Witch"

E. Reid Gilbert

An Irish poet, James Liddy, called Edna Kritz Meudt, a "literary witch because of her intuition for personal sorcery."

Valley Studio was right across the creek from Edna's home place and adjacent to her grandparents Kritz's homestead. The one-room Kritz School, where Edna received her early education, was less than a mile up the Upper Wyoming road from us. Actually, we bought the schoolhouse, moved it to our campus, painted it brown and used it for a ballet studio, fully utilizing its hardwood maple floor.

First meeting Edna at the Uplands Arts Council art gallery barn, I was mesmerized by her poetry readings. She was accompanied by her fourteen-year-old grandson, Chris, who was also her ward. Her poem, "The Summer Day That Changed the World," introduced me not only to her and her life, but also the creative energy of the *Valley of the God Almighty Joneses* (Frank Lloyd Wright's family) as well as the tragedy of the 1914 murders at Taliesin.

In her poem about Taliesin she recorded the events of that fateful day through her eight-year-old eyes. It seems that she had been invited to a birthday party for Margaret Cheney who was visiting her mother, Mamah Borthwick (Frank Lloyd Wright's mistress) for the summer. A psychotic servant, Julian, heeding the voice in his head, had locked all the doors of the dining room, then set the place on fire while everyone was having lunch. Whoever was able to escape the fire was met with a hatchet outside the one unlocked door. Five adults and three children lost their lives that day. Edna was lucky to have arrived late.

When Edna was already a published poet, she and a Wisconsin historian were inspecting the graveyard at Unity Chapel, the family church of the Lloyd Joneses and the Lloyd Wrights. As they approached Mamah's gravestone, the historian said, "I wonder if anyone knows who is buried here."

Edna replied, "I certainly should. I was there the day she died. . . .I've been thinking about writing a story about that."

"Oh, no! You can't write a story about such a horrific event."

No one should ever tell Edna what she couldn't do. She wrote the story but discovered that prose didn't capture the drama or the emotion of the tragedy. Her poetry did. Her reflections of the events were captured at the end of her poem in these lines:

> *O generations! – Whatever it is we are –*
> *never the same after some ruined hill is climbed*
> *and we meet face to face the Thing that makes it Was.*

The apprentices at Valley Studio were always pleased whenever I invited Edna to share some of her poetry with us in front of the fireplace in the common room.

They, being a part of the '70s generation, were intrigued with the poems of her farm life, but more particularly of her love life.

As a teenager, she was deemed ready—by her parents—for matrimony, so they arranged for her to marry Peter Meudt, a successful farmer near Dodgeville, fifteen miles away and several years older. She seemed to sum up this portion of her life with one phrase from her poem, *The Round River Canticle*:

> *Auctioned to an unfriendly world . . .*

Although she was in an arranged marriage, she was not devoid of love. Many of her poems chronicled this love, much to the embarrassment of her children and grandchildren. Her response to them was, "A poet is honest if nothing else."

The object of her love was a Roman Catholic priest who

reflected her love in his own emotional life. However, they both had vows—she, her marriage vows and he, his priestly vows—vows which they never violated. Even in their reciprocal love letters, they remained circumspect.

Father Dan spent the last five years of his life—while in declining health with cancer—in the home of Edna and Peter. Then, after the deaths of Peter, Edna and Father Dan, whenever I visit the house—currently the home of her grandson, Chris—the room where the Right Reverend Daniel Coyne died is referred to as "Father Dan's room."

Of all Edna's poems dedicated to Father Dan or celebrating their love, the most poignant is "I Most Regret" :

> *I most regret never having danced with you*
> *To ever-pervading music in a ballroom never seen.*
> *. . . When I slip through*
> *O dance me toward the Sun!*

One Saturday August morning, at the end of the first week of a new studio session of fresh new faces and energies, I called Edna to invite her for afternoon tea later that day. She readily agreed, and then we chatted about sundry things. Before hanging up she said, "Reid, you know my acceptance to your invitation is contingent."

I replied, "Contingent upon what?"

"Oh . . . an act of God or a natural disaster!"

"Edna, why do you always say things like that? Of course I would understand if something drastic were to happen before then."

After the phone call, the school cook served a scrumptious lunch, as usual, in the dining hall. At about two o'clock I saw an ominous cloud south of us in the Dodgeville direction. In about thirty minutes the phone rang. I knew it was Edna.

When I picked up the phone and greeted the caller, Edna calmly said, "This is Edna."

"Yes, I know! What happened?"

She answered, "I'll have to cancel the invitation. A tornado just hit here, taking down several trees, breaking tree branches and pushing the barn off its foundation. I'm particularly distressed that the larch tree at the side of the yard was uprooted. It was at least 100 years old, and I've always been so fond of it."

After a few more exchanges, I said, "We'll be there tomorrow morning to help you clean up."

"That would be wonderful."

The next morning the mime actors and students trekked to Edna's to clear up the debris from the storm. We couldn't do anything about the barn, and she had already arranged for a construction company to send a crane the next day to upright her beloved larch.

One of our new apprentices, Cleatius Gouldman, was Jewish and Blackfeet Indian. He looked at the upended root ball of the larch and asked, "Edna do you have any clean white sheets which you would allow to be torn up?"

"Yes, I do."

She then yelled at Chris, "Chris, get that old sheet I washed on Monday."

Chris brought the sheet, and Cleatius ripped the sheet into two-inch wide strips, which he then tied around the root ends now exposed to the air.

Edna watched studiously and asked, "Cleatius, why did you do that?"

"That was so that the tree spirit would know we haven't abandoned it."

Although Edna is no longer among the living, the larch has made it into the new century.

Edna left Wyoming Valley
Before the Wisconsin Mime Theatre and School
Found it.
Meetings were coffee and saffron bread occasions
With rumorings and apparitions and contradictions
But no dogmas
Never dogmas.
We choreographed her Round River Canticle
To discover that she had not completely left the valley;
She keeps flowing back.
The round river epitomizes her poetry
Which spurts into politics and historical figures and
Images to reflow or
Reflower through herself

Edna entertaining the troupes

Vet Student Fulfills Mother's Dying Wish

Cleatius Gouldman

If you have not met Cleatius Gouldman, it is likely you have at least caught sight of him strolling across campus. He has a few uniquely identifiable features that distinguish him from most students: his signature sprawling white beard; his black MIA/POW cap that is weathered, faded and frayed on the edges of the brim; and a laptop bag bearing a few small splatters of paint that offer a subtle clue to his academic major.

In 1975-77 he studied and performed at the Valley Studio with the Wisconsin Mime Theatre and School.

His education was interrupted by work, travel, music and art. Gouldman is a native of downstate Niles. He returned to Michigan in 1993 to care for his ailing mother. His final promise before she died was that he would complete his degree.

"My morri loved artwork," said Gouldman, who is soft-spoken and exceptionally polite (his interview responses are laced with "Yes, ma'am"). "She pretty much taught me how to draw. She also taught me how to play basketball. I could never beat her because she had a set shot that she let fly halfway across the court. I was a single child and our family went to church every night when I was young. That's where I learned how to draw. It was a good way to babysit me and keep me quiet-give me something to doodle on.

"It feels wonderful to get my degree. I don't believe I could have accomplished it without the assistance of the people at Northern.

From professors to secretaries to custodians, they're all just wonderful, helpful and respectful."

Gouldman served in the U.S. Army from 1968-1971 during the Cold War. In an effort to develop advanced air-defense capability to neutralize a potential attack by Soviet bombers, the United States produced a series of Nike anti-aircraft missiles. Gouldman's assignment revolved around the Nike Hercules missile.

"I activated and deactivated nuclear warheads," he said. "Life carries a lot of stress for veterans. I started having seizures. When I got back into art, I realized it was the stress causing those physical problems because the seizures diminished. Art is a healing process."

The piece Gouldman has on display in the senior exhibition is an abstract medley of some scraps of poetry based on his military experience, red to reflect the blood of a Cold War memory, broken CDs to envision the energy of his personal chakra, and landscapes to reflect freedom from his past. He credits retiring Art and Design professor John Hubbard and former professor M'olfram Niessen for their support and inspiration. Gouldman said he was honored to work with Niessen on the concrete sculpture in front of Lee Hall in the '70s.

When he left NMU early the first time around, Gouldman went to Wisconsin and assisted Frank Lloyd Wright Taliesin Fellows with home restorations. He later spent 25 years on Vashon Island near Seattle, working in construction and immersing himself in the rock 'n' roll scene via different bands. After graduation, he plans to someday return to the Seattle area and get back into a former love: theater. He's working on an original musical based on late author Carson McCullers' novel, The Ballad of Sad Cafe. The Southern blues-flavored songs he's written for the show include "Eagle Don't Cluck Like a Chicken," "Nobody Sings Face Down" and "Sharecropper's Blues." A sample lyric follows:

> Bring back memories for my winter months
> It's spring time returning and butterflies' rebirth
> And your painted wing will be glowing

Just retracing time when our love was flowering ...
Hanging heavy on the vine

Beneath the MIA/POW logo, on the right side of the brim of the well-worn cap, is stitched the phrase, "You Are Not Forgotten." It is an appropriate sentiment-not only in deference to Gouldman's military service, but because some at NMU will not soon forget his memorable personality, stories and visible presence on campus.

Snowflake

Gale LaJoye

The last time I spoke in character on stage was in 1973 in a production of "One Flew Over the Cuckoo's Nest" where I played Randle Patrick McMurphy. It was my third year attending Northern Michigan University in Marquette Michigan. I still hadn't declared a major but most of my classes were in the art department. During that time I was considering something in design, utilitarian or environmental, and fulfilling the required basics courses. When given the choice between taking another humanities class or Intro to Theatre – I chose the later. One of the requirements of the class was to try out for one of the semester's theatre productions. I struggled through my first auditions and eventually landed a part in Chekhov's, Three Sisters, playing the part of the good doctor Ivan Romanovich Chebutykin.

Back then, I was working a construction job by day, taking classes and acting in plays by night. I found this to be perfect research for playing a character like McMurphy, my final role at Northern Michigan University. With thirteen hundred dollars saved up I decided I was going to make it or break it. I responded to an ad in Dance Magazine for the Wisconsin Mime School in Spring Green Wisconsin. They were offering a summer workshop. I talked with my co-actor, Cleatius Gouldman who played Chief Bromden in Cuckoo's Nest into signing up and we headed to Wisconsin and the Valley Studio for the summer.

I remember some pretty magical nights at the studio. One night in particular, I was walking along the dirt road and a fog started to roll in and blanket the valley just when the fireflies were coming out. The whole valley looked like a huge city far off in the distance. No traffic sounds only the city lights blinking on and off. The whole experience seemed foreign and exotic. I was only a few hundred miles away from the Upper Peninsula of Michigan but I felt like I was in a distant land.

The summer workshop was a great introduction to various theatre and movement disciplines, pantomime, mime, Commedia dell' Arte, acting classes and a workshop on movement technique in Japanese Kabuki Theatre. During my workshops and before my solo performances I still incorporate the isolation exercises I learned in the pantomime class.

One exercise stands out the most. At the beginning of the day, we were given a small towel and asked to spread out in the room, and get down on our hands and knees and wipe the floor around us to define our "sacred" performance space. I was skeptical and thought this was a clever way to get the floor cleaned. However, a few years later I used that exercise while teaching at Ringling Brothers & Barnum and Bailey Clown College as a method of improvisation and character development with beginning students. Classes were conducted in the middle of a large arena of a 42 foot circus ring, not exactly an intimate space for improv. I wanted the space to feel more intimate and thought back to the "defining your space" exercise. I did not ask them to get down on their hands and knees with a towel but I did ask them to treat the ring as a "sacred space" and only enter, sustain and exit in character.

After the summer workshop was over, Cleatius stayed on and I returned to Marquette with eight hundred dollars still in my pocket. Upon my return, a friend of mine told me about the Ringling Brothers & Barnum and Bailey Clown College in Venice Florida and I gave them a call. I knew the application process was over but I decided to try anyway. As luck would have it, Bill Ballantine, Dean of Ringling Brothers & Barnum and Bailey Clown College, left some openings for promising late comers. When I told him I just finished a summer workshop at the Wisconsin Mime School, he said he was looking for someone with mime training to round out the student body that year.

I felt this was an opportunity to build on what I already experienced at the Valley Studio. I never considered a career as a clown in the circus. The course was eight weeks long. During that time, we studied circus techniques, pantomime, mime and character improvisations, dance and movement, different genre of physical comedy from circus to silent film, even yoga and nutrition.

At the conclusion of studies and performances at Ringling Brothers & Barnum and Bailey Clown College, I was offered a contract with the Blue Unit. I felt there was a lot of opportunity in the field of clowning compared to the overcrowded mime world. The older clowns were retiring, others had passed away and the new ones were not yet established in the art form in the United States.

Just before Christmas, I arrived back home in Marquette, six months after beginning my quest with exactly one nickel in my pocket and a contract to be a clown in the "Greatest Show on Earth". I stopped at one of my favorite haunts in college to celebrate. It was 25 cents for a beer – I had to borrow 20 cents! The next day I sold my Dodge Coronet for enough money to buy my plane ticket back to Florida.

I spent six years with Ringling Brothers Circus. I started out as a "First of May Clown" with the blue unit, a "Boss Clown" at Ringling Brothers Circus World, then "Master Clown Instructor" at the Clown College, before ballyhooing the circus as an "Advance Clown". In 1979 after a couple of years as the Director of Theatre Operations at Circus World, I left to pursue a career on stage, producing and performing silent comedy one man shows nationally and internationally. As one thing leads to another, if I hadn't attended the summer workshop at the Valley Studio I wouldn't have gone on to Clown College and I would have never pursued the art of clowning and solo performances as a lifetime career.

That was 43 years ago. I'm currently celebrating my twenty-fifth anniversary tour of my show *Snowflake*. A word-less one man performance, which has toured throughout Asia, Australia,

Mexico, Canada and the United States, Scotland, Ireland and Hong Kong. In Japan alone *Snowflake* toured to 300 cities with over 400 performances.

Currently I'm working on a staged memoir about my work, travels, and experiences throughout the years, part truth but mostly fiction. After years of work mastering the art of gesture, silent communication, and poignant story telling, I think I'm going to have to find my voice again.

LaJoye up a tree

More Than a Place

Grant Bashore

When you are eight years old the world is a much bigger place. In the mind that is. And when you are asked more than four decades later to relive it, suddenly the names of those beings that shared your space, the trees that grew around you, and the "whys" and "how comes", all the *reasons* for things, well they just don't all fit anymore into one neat little corner of the mind's cupboard. To complicate matters, important events in our lives often generate reflections for years afterwards. And some of those reflections take on the feeling of original memories, begging the question: what is real? I went back to Spring Green, Wisconsin in my fifties to be sure, and everything fell into that eerie zone of distant familiarity. Trees were in the same place, but so much bigger. The cheese factory was there, but with a different name and purpose. And the barns all looked older or were since gone, cattails and milkweed now filling in their foundations. So to be clear, what I am about to tell you will necessarily lack all the names of those that made me happy, the backstories that put things in their right context, and the magical efforts that got us all to one place for three summers in a row. But that place was real. And the images, well they pepper my mind to this day with inspiration. The Valley Studio in Spring Green, Wisconsin was the place: an upheaval of creative coincidence nestled between the political mayhem of the sixties and everyone's new hope for seventies liberation. But to this kid, there could have been no better place in time.

Dr. E. Reid Gilbert got me there. And my mother. She marched me down my first theatre steps after Reid performed a solo mime show in Madison. I was seven. I wanted to meet the "mime-man". And lo and behold, suddenly there he was with wild hair, a sweat-stained performance shirt, and streaks of missed whiteface on one jaw.

Later, after years of training, I would come to respect the art of mime as a never-ending companion. I'd begin to move beyond technique; and, as in life, face the challenges of reduction, economy, and letting go. I tried to go the way of others' expectations. I became a successful lawyer. I married. I had children. I divorced. I held a dying parent (that same mother). In short, I felt the pull and painful extraction that life's chapters sometimes dish up. But this is no rant. Throughout all, I held close to the art, the art that the "mime-man" and Valley Studio put in me. And this has made me a better person.

So there I was, looking up at two people who held my destiny. And when Reid said to my mother, "Yes, we can make an exception and allow your son to join the adult school," I really had no idea what I was in for.

The entrance was a long, gravel driveway that rounded one bend of trees to reveal the first set of buildings. I remember entering the renovated barn that served as the studio. Downstairs the fieldstone foundation was cold and rough, and it walled in several sleeping quarters. But as you ascended the stairs you entered a light-filled room full of possibility. It was the place where I would learn to balance, spin, walk in place, and meditate. It was the place where I would begin to know my body. It housed the floor on which I would later rest as a companion placed cold, wet strips of casting bandage on my face to create my first mask. It was the place I snuck out to late at night because I wanted to be with the Taiwanese shadow puppeteers. I joined them in their large room, and they would laugh big laughs when I performed a few illusions. And they shared the secrets of their craft, flipping open the locks of a large brown travel crate, revealing slim flat figurines that with a touch of light became gods in the woods. We did all this for hours and without the benefit of a common language. Without knowing it, I was already travelling the world.

Between the studio and the farmhouse was a large sunflower. I'd sit with the Gilbert's black-haired dog "Smokey", my new friend, and pick fallen seeds out of his coat. Sometimes, Reid's daughter Karen, who was younger, would join me. We would greet the early sun and pet our dog together, a real thrill to a young boy who, having grown up in a family of four sons, knew nothing about girls.

On the other side of the sunflower was the main house. Here I would learn to play my first chords on a piano and sing (thank you Carlos Moser). It was everyone's grandmother's living room: curtained windows, wood floors, a large rug. The place to just hang out. Downstairs was an apartment, and the man that lived there let me play my first favorite song on his record player, over and over again. It was Cat Steven's "Wild World", and even though life would later teach me that "it's hard to get by just upon a smile," the Valley Studio was going to give me, like it or not, many smiles first.

I say "like it or not" because there was a necessary discipline to the Valley Studio (we just called it: "The Studio") that kept things running. Reid was an uncompromising artist. And when something didn't work, he let you know about it. There was a time to get up. A time to report for kitchen duty. A time to go to sleep. To a young boy free of his parents, brothers, and the city, this was not all peaches and cream. But herein is the gift: I learned at an early age that discipline can leave time for life to unfold. And unfold it did those summers.

We rode in the back of a hearse into town for performances. Someone had the fun idea to paint our faces ahead of time and pull back the black curtains as cars passed us on the highway, shocking the local farmers right out of their bib overalls. The Gard Theatre in the village of Spring Green was a mysterious place, and I explored the backstage alleyways filled with thick ropes, large levers, sandbags, and old lights with a sense of performer's privilege. Underneath the main stage was the green room, and the place, amidst the dust and haze of a purple stage lamp, where I caught my first glimpse of a grown – woman's breast. You see, being only eight years of age amidst a co-ed group of performers conferred on me certain privileges the grown men of the troupe did not enjoy. I was no threat to the women; and in a lovely, non-sexual way, I was invited along on all-female swims in the Wisconsin River, an event that inevitably involved nudity. I would return to The Studio only to find a cadre of frustrated men encircling me, their huddled and hushed voices begging me to tell them what happened. With the supreme sense of power only eight-year-olds can muster, I would respond: "oh, if you only knew!" And when they wept for more, I would only add to their suffering and state: "Are you kidding, I saw much more than that!" I would later harness that early sense of power, taking the center stage floodlight as I portrayed Snoopy on top of his doghouse, shooting down the lightning-speed Luftwaffe around him—all silently, of course.

Yes, there is power in mime. And as mime artists we are constantly trying to find that perfect flash-point where thought and emotion meet movement. Mime functions best when the bedrock of presence is undisturbed. And presence relies on a certain authenticity of energy. Whenever life has caught me walking with head and body separate, or worse, with head and body united but spirit blown apart, I come back to the practice of mime. Because the creation of an authentic moment of silent energy commands psycho-physical integrity, it is the perfect art for re-assembly. Once mind-body authenticity is regained, you just add a drop of breath-spirit, and the magic ripples. The community of The Studio instilled all this in me. It is a lifetime gift.

So what else was The Studio? Well, it grew quickly, I remember that. There was construction and dorms that appeared farther up on the hill. A sewage system that I vaguely recall caused some internal political bickering. But the spirit outlived these growing pains, and the place, to me, remains a litany of "firsts."

On one outing to the "Ratskeller" barn, I saw my first luna moth. We ventured outside despite the warning drops of an oncoming storm. It's emerald presence later inspired a Haiku:

Luna moth sits still
On gray, barn wood sill. Look here!
Lightning speaks my name.

I listened to my first whip-poor-will song. It floated over to us from the hill opposite the outdoor stage we built for evening performances and feedback. I sat in a teepee. The humid smell of canvas and the grass floor provided a cool place for secrets on hot afternoons. I gazed at the Northern Lights, undulating green and pink tendrils that caressed us into silence. I caught fireflies, spotted a raccoon, and took mock "airplane" rides. There was someone playing a dulcimer, and Reid made a skinny wooden puppet dance with a stick. There was a kind man that lived off-site in a geodesic dome. On special days, we ate batter-fried day lilies together.

When performances neared there was the smell of white powder in a tied-up sock and leather-soled movement shoes with the thin black tongue (does anyone make them anymore?). There was the pleasantly cold touch of a black-liner pencil as someone circled the outer edge of my face paint, and the easy feeling of cold cream remover after a job well-done. The discarded makeup tissues stained red and white that lay on the floor were a symbol of our communion, throw-away bandages that allowed us to heal ourselves by healing others.

Yes, The Studio was more than a place to learn the performing arts. To the adults, I suppose it was a place where one could press life's reset button. Jugglers, clowns, actors, musicians, and wandering yogis were all welcomed. My schizophrenic cousin came one summer and performed a magic show. My father, recently divorced and homeless, spent one winter there. The Studio was like that you see. Everyone was welcomed to visit. And if you could make a case for your creative needs, you were often invited to stay. And to me, it was the place where the world first opened up and invited a young boy to explore.

Before her death, my mother shared something with me. She told me that it pained her deeply to pick me up after each eight-week summer session at The Studio. Apparently, I would weep the entire 45-minute ride back to Madison. And through those tears, I would beg for her understanding: "But mom, *those* are my friends, and *that* is my home." Strangely, I do not remember this very clearly. Nor do I remember all my friends' names. But you all are still a happy part of me. That's what happens I suppose when the gifts of a place outdo the fleeting pains. I held my mother's hand before her passing, and I thanked her for her courage. She let me return to The Studio three summers in a row. Everyone should be so lucky.

Maybe that's what the "E" in E. Reid Gilbert stands for. Everyone. Together. Growing in Art. As for me, well I'll just go on stringing these magical moments one after another on the necklace of life. I think, in the end, that's as close to eternity as you can get.

—Grant Bashore
(June 22, 2015)

Addendum

The airplane ride to which Grant is referring was a simple game of perception, although at the time, we didn't lecture about it.

The mock airplane was simply a four-foot-long board laid across a stick, which served as a fulcrum, thus in a crude sense the shape of an airplane. The passenger was blindfolded, led to step on top of the wings and told to "Hold on!" As he held onto the top of a person's head in front of the plane, two people (one on each end of the wing) began to raise the aerial conveyance. But they raised it no more than a couple of inches above the plane fuselage, as the helpful person in front began slowly to descend.

When the passenger felt he was several feet off the ground, the wingtippers began to wiggle the wing as though they were losing control. Someone would yell, "Jump, Grant," a command which he obediently responded to. He was quite surprised when the grassy ground met him much quicker than he expected. He and all the conspirators collapsed in laughter.

At the beginning of each new session, Grant would insist that we give some new unsuspecting passenger a ride. After several of these seemingly initiation rites, and a new victim had taken a ride, Grant said, "I want to take the ride again."

I said, "Grant, it won't be the same, as you already know what it is." He kept insisting, so we blindfolded him. With an air of complete confidence, he stepped onto the plane wing with very little assistance.

As he began his airplane ride, he continued his air of self-assurance. I had been able to get the message to the wing lifters that they should actually raise him as high as they could. He, of course, thought the person whose head he was attached to was descending. At the top height of his flight, we yelled, "Jump Grant." He stepped cockily off the airplane, but immediately was flailing through space. He had expected to be on the ground immediately, but was utterly surprised as he parachuted through the air and was caught by the onlookers. When he removed his blindfold, he was still wide-eyed in amazement. He was sure that he knew where he was in his new flight.

As much fun as the game was, it was also a wonderful experience of perception. The first-timers perceived that they were rising several feet off the ground. Grant had perceived the same thing on his maiden voyage (a perception with misinformation). Even on his second flight, his perception was based on what he thought he already knew and was surprised to discover he was fooled again because of a fixed notion of reality.

Perhaps an existential lesson!

erg

Grant Bashore began mime studies in the 1970's with Dr. E. Reid Gilbert at the Wisconsin Mime Theatre and Valley Studio in Spring Green, Wisconsin. At the Valley Studio Grant studied yoga, character acting, mime, mask, dance, and voice. At age10 he performed his first mime skits before a live audience at the Gard Theater in Spring Green, Wisconsin and landed the lead of Amal in the opera *Amal and The Night Visitors*. Grant interned two summers at the School for Mime Theatre at Kenyon College in Gambier,

Ohio; and he has studied with Steve Wasson and Corrine Soum of the International School of Corporeal Mime (London/Spring Green). Grant completed a four-year residency of study with Philip G. Bennett (teaching assistant to Sonia Moore) in the Stanislavsky system of acting. Grant is also an instructor in the Stanislavsky Method of Physical Actions. As a result, Grant represents a unique talent in both the stylized world of silent theatre and the speaking "theatre of living experience". He has performed with Tucson Theatrical Mime Theatre, and the Improv Comedy Troupes "Jester'Z" (Phoenix) and "Not Burned Out Just Unscrewed" (Tucson). He also appears in solo mime shows throughout the country. Stage credits include Cheswick in *One Flew Over the Cuckoo's Nest* (2000 <u>Zoni</u> Award, Theater Works); Lord Capulet in *Romeo and Juliet* (Tucson Community Theater); Judas in *Frida Kahlo* (Teatro Bravo); the Duke in *Measure for Measure* (Tucson Theatre Ensemble) and Arthur in *The Balcony* (Rogue Theatre). Grant is a member of the Screen Actor's Guild and AEA. He lives in Tucson, Arizona.

Coordination of Body Parts: Reid Gilbert's mime classs

If There Were Ever a Place

Tari Lynn Gilbert

If there were ever a place, a physical place, which imprinted deeply on me, it would be Valley Studio. I've lived many places in my life, thanks in my childhood to my adventurous father who instilled curiosity in my soul. I've experienced many different cultures and all have something wonderful to recommend them, but of all the places I've lived, Valley Studio is singular in its call to me, deep as the summer whip-o-will.

Valley Studio was my father's dream, perhaps his noblest child, and a lovely dream it was. Nestled in the rolling hills in the driftless southwestern part of Wisconsin, the Studio had both a modern post-Wright feel to it, as well as ghosts in those hills. Legend had it that the Native peoples did not live in this particular valley, because it was too sacred. That feeling remained, even many years after they had been removed from the area. There was something about the Studio that ushered in a kind of reverence in people approaching it for the first time. Something I still feel, if I venture on its lands, although it has now become a hunting ground for a rich businessman. This pains me, as the echoes of mid-summer night performances still ring through for me.

I spent my summers, from ages 10 to 15, at the Studio. My experiences were not all of one sort. In the earlier days, my sisters and I slept in the old farmhouse, awakened at night by ghosts playing the piano or moving furniture. We moved up as the Studio grew, and my last summer was spent above the schoolhouse, in a makeshift loft with several wild women (wasn't the Studio full of those?). I participated in many performances, wove daisy chains while watching others, learned how to wash a milk glass (cold water, thank you very much), made masks, made stories, made friends. I lost some innocence, and gained some sense of myself that remains with me to this day.

One night in particular that stands out for me was a night when Aurora Borealis blessed us with her colours. This was part of the magic there—one never knew what was coming, but it was bound to be extraordinary. I'd seen quite beautiful northern lights there before, but on this particular night the sky pulsated with colours— greens, pinks, blue. I lay on the front lawn with Dana Burgess and we were speechless, just experiencing the light show that nature had bestowed on us. As the dew settled in, crickets chirping, and the colours faded, we gathered our belongings and headed to our respective bunks, bound by a spectacle that few people ever have an opportunity to witness. Although our own performances were often quite professional, especially considering how quickly they coalesced from idea to stage, nature had the triumphant show, particularly that night.

Once upon a time, there was a school of mime, in a hidden valley, in a secret and sacred space. That school, that time, that was special.

Ghosts at the Studio

Adrienne Gilbert Ramirez

Valley Studio played a big part in my early life. The people I met and the experiences I had spending so many summers at the studio in the outdoors, bohemian environment have stayed with me for decades now. I have memories of walking all the way to the Wisconsin River to swim, crazy! Hours of rambling hikes in the woods and of course a variety of different classes and characters.

One thing that remained relatively consistent over the years at Valley Studio was the unexpected and random ghostly sighting. The first summer that we were at Valley Studio, when the buildings consisted of just the house and barn, before the dorms were built I had my 'first ghost encounter'.

It was in the old farm house. It was a beautiful dwelling in the luscious green, but rumored to be haunted valley. During the first years my sisters, Tari and Karen and I were often the only children around during evening gatherings.

The building we lived in that summer at Valley Studio was the farm house which had been renovated into a larger space to accommodate socializing and cooking. In this new modern space was a beautiful shiny black piano that captured my attention. It was like no piano I had seen before; it was sleek like it should be in an upscale apartment. Yet it was out in the middle of the country at Valley Studio.

One night in the middle of our first Valley Studio summer, Tari and I were woken up by piano music, along with people singing and talking. The sounds of the festive party carried up the stairs to our room. We were surprised by what we heard because we remembered everyone heading off to bed at about the same time.

After several minutes of fidgeting and trying to decipher conversations to figure out who was visiting, Tari and I decided to investigate. We knew we'd probably get into some trouble, but we'd also get a chance to say hello which would, no doubt be followed by a quick 'good night'.

We slowly went down the hall and descended down the stairs, as the music continued we were careful to move slowly thinking that our deliberate progression would muffle the sounds of our descent. As soon as we could see into the living room everything fell silent. The room was completely empty. The piano was closed. It was dark and no one was there to scold us for getting up.

Our surprise quickly changed to fear, the hair on the back of our necks tingled and we leapt up the stairs to our beds. We pulled the covers over our heads and the warmth provided us with a feeling of safety.

The next morning we shared the story and learned we were the only ones who heard anything.

Every summer that I returned to Valley Studio I would see a ghost. Usually they appeared between the old farm house and dorms up the hill. But never again was I with anyone else, nor was it as shocking and memorable as my initial ghostly experience.

William Burdick's ballet class

My Story Is Very Different

Karen Gilbert

My story is very different from most. I did not work hard to get to Valley Studio, it was not my dream, or my passion, it was what I was born into. From about the age of 7 until I was 15 I spent my summers at the studio, because I am Reid's youngest daughter. My childhood memory is not very good, I rely a lot on my sisters to fill in the gaps, but I will do my best to dig deep and remember, all these years later.

As I said everyone else who was at Valley Studio wanted to be there so much. I am sure I was the only one who skipped classes. I didn't have a talent I was trying to refine and grow, I was a kid. I just wanted to be outside with my dogs. We spent hours up in the woods, hiking and just being together.

I remember the ghost in the dorm and the house foundation up in the hills. The house was long gone, abandoned and fallen apart. The story was that a family lived up there and the husband killed his wife and mother in-law. We all assumed that the ghost was one of the women from that house. It was a scary story, but somehow I never actually felt scared of her, maybe because I had my protector Smokey with me most of the time.

Smokey was my baby, my best friend, my constant companion. Still when I dream that I am in danger a black lab is there to make sure I am safe. I assume it is Smokey still protecting me. I also remember the whippoor-will, who would sing at night. Sometimes it would be so quiet and dark that I felt like I could be the last living thing on earth. But then I would hear her up in the hills and I knew I wasn't alone. She was very comforting.

I did enjoy my classes too. It just wasn't the same as for other people I'm sure, but I learned some useful things. I can use the isolation techniques to help my yoga practice, or anything physical that I do. I can also impress people when I show off those unique talents. Not many people are able to bend one finger at a time or rotate their elbow without moving their hand.

A couple of years ago I went to a meditation retreat just down hwy 23 from the Studio. It was a silent retreat, and was an amazing experience for me. I was able to wander around in those beautiful woods again, and if I came across anyone, I didn't even need to talk to them. I could just nod and continue in my own world, in my own head through my old woods. The only thing missing was Smokey, and I missed him terribly. I realized that weekend how lucky I was to have had that experience. The area is so magical and beautiful and I got to spend my childhood with it as my playground.

Smokey, a dog for all seasons

Valley Studio Memoir
Michael Pedretti

I came to Valley Studio in 1977 or 1978 in search of understanding of how movement could more effectively be used on stage to make a performance jump off the stage onto the audience's lap. I was not disappointed. I took only three classes, one each from Reid Gilbert, Tom Leabhart and Marjorie Barstow. Reid simplified the complexity of movement and made it immediately accessible and meaningful to me. Tom demonstrated the value of controlled and explosive movement. Barstow captured the essence of being one with the moment and the movement. It was a transformative experience as a teacher of acting, a director of theater plays, a writer and a thinker.

I did not come to Valley Studio because of any special interest in mime or clown, but I left with an awareness of the power of both to transform an audience. It would be an understatement to say that I was transformed by the experiences of that summer from both the classes and the performances that took place in the open air.

That summer and consequent work with Reid Gilbert led to my work in the mime and clown field, producing a handful of international festivals, national conferences and over a dozen years of summer workshops.

The Beginning of My Creative Life
Sande Zeig

The Valley Studio marked the beginning of my creative life in so many ways. Dr. E. Reid Gilbert is an inspiring mentor and teacher. His extensive knowledge of theatrical traditions including Noh and Kabuki from Japan as well as the work of Marcel Marceau and Etienne Decroux in Paris nourished us and opened our imaginations. He sang songs from his childhood in The Appalachian Mountains. He taught us the art of storytelling. He taught us everything he knew, including about the lone whippoorwill that would sing everyday at dusk. He gave us infinite room to grow creatively— both as a group and individually.

After rigorous training with Reid, I created sketches and performed duos with my close friends at the studio, Heather Wallace and Karil Kirk. Heather and I did a piece called "Gravity" and Karil and I did a reinterpretation of the Garden of Eden story called "Lilith." Then Reid invited me to start traveling and performing with him. This was a great honor and I have treasured memories from being on the road with him.

Reid spoke with such affection and enthusiasm about his studies with Marcel Marceau's teacher, Etienne Decroux, that I decided to study with him in Paris in 1973. I studied with him for a year. During that year I found "les Feminist Revolutionaries" and met Monique Wittig, a renowned French novelist and visionary, with whom I lived and collaborated with on books, plays and films for almost thirty years.

Reid's guidance, mentoring and big heart have stayed with me throughout the years. My two years at the Valley Study were the foundation for my life as an artist. Reid gave us confidence, love and creative freedom to grow, explore and expand. I am forever grateful to all the students I met and worked with at the Valley Studio, especially Heather and Karil, and above all, I am grateful to Reid, a shining light on my path.

Sande Zeig and Heather Wallace in GRAVITY

Four Main Memories

Chuck Kleymeyer

First is Reid Gilbert showing students how not to carry an imaginary (or stage-prop) suitcase: "Watch me lift it with just my forearm and then swing it back and forth with my wrist—after all, it's EMPTY, just like all suitcases that people lift and walk off with... right?" Then he would tell us why every stage and movie actor needed mime training, because of this kind of lack of knowledge of how humans interact with the material (real) world.

Some years after I was a student at Valley Studio, Reid Gilbert visited Washington, D.C., where I was working as a writer and as a cultural sociologist for a foundation that supports international grassroots development. Reid gave me a call and I suggested we go to the magnificent Auguste Rodin exhibit at the National Gallery of Art – East Wing on the National Mall. I have never forgotten that visit with Reid, and I've recreated it for many, many people since then. Reid and I moved from sculpture to sculpture, discussing each work of art as someone trained as a mime would see it. How Rodin captured motion and power, despair and tenderness, in an immobile object. The Walking Man, The Age of Bronze, Balzac, The Kiss, St. John the Baptist, The Burghers of Calais—all of them came alive for me in a way I had never experienced them before. My concept of Rodin, and of all sculptors, was changed for life. Later, when I wrote my book, YESHU: A Novel for the Open-Hearted, I incorporated Michelangelo, Rodin, Gargallo, and other artists into my descriptions of characters and scenes. My novel has won three national awards, and this kind of word and image-sculpting is one of the reasons.

Finally, I remember the poetic and whimsical, but totally serious, Tom Leabhart as he taught his Corporal Mime class. We would warm up every session with the well-known Shaker dancing song, "Simple Gifts." Just read the lyrics below and imagine Tom and all of us students flowing slowly and gracefully, forwards and backwards, to these words:

> 'Tis the gift to be simple, 'tis the gift to be free
> 'Tis the gift to come down where we ought to be,
> And when we find ourselves in the place just right,
> 'Twill be in the valley of love and delight.
> When true simplicity is gain'd,
> To bow and to bend we shan't be asham'd,
> To turn, turn will be our delight,
> Till by turning, turning we come 'round right.

I also vividly remember Tom Leabhart demonstrating the essential difference between Einstein and Elvis: "Head thrust forward. Like this!...Pelvis thrust forward. Like that!" No need to exaggerate it. Be the difference.

At the Valley Studio 1972–1974

Lauren Carley

I studied mime with Reid Gilbert at the Valley Studio between 1972 and 1974. I was running away from a lonely stint, living in Germany and threw myself into the community living and daily study of mime with relieved joy.

I slept in the one-room schoolhouse's attic, which, like a haymow, was hot and strewn with bits and pieces of straw, boxes and families of field mice, which had no problem running over my head at night. I wrote my adolescent poetry up there, experienced my first passionate lovemaking. The window had no curtain and I slept easily and quietly in the breeze that came through. The moon shone through that window, along with the stars, and when there was no moon, it was a black darkness that is rarely seen anymore. For we were truly in a rural valley without street lights, surrounded by woods and fields.

Reid was *laissez faire* with our "activities" so long as we studied, fulfilled our community duties and didn't get into too much trouble with the local bartenders. He was so tolerant. I was finishing an undergrad degree in vocal music and he let me practice (often quite loudly) my opera arias at his upright piano in his own cottage. I'm sure it didn't provide for a quiet lunch for him.

My first year at Valley Studio was learning the introductory physical aspects of mime: body, makeup, silence. We became actors in space, and learned to charge the space around and between us with a meaning that didn't involve words. We strengthened, toned, maneuvered because every move was meaning. The index finger lifting in space had meaning. It gave me a sense of personal power, a sovereignty I hadn't experienced before.

During the summer, Reid hired teachers from around the world to teach us more about the physical self: karate, Indian dance, Commedia, Lecoq and Decroux mime styles, improvisation and status. We were privileged to have full days of both learning and performance. After hours, we laughed and explored one another, cooking, creating, making love, being stupid and young and carefree.

There was a cadre of young, political lesbians at the Studio in those days, which adjured me to get rid of my eye make-up and bra, don the "outfit" of the era: overalls or painter's pants and t-shirt, which we wore when we weren't in leotards. In the second year I was at the Studio, our little cadre of "women-identified women" created a piece which we called LILITH based on the Lilith myth. It was for International Women's Day, March 8, 1974. It ended, by the way, with Lilith kissing Eve. The place, filled with Madison women, erupted. I created the role of SNAKE in this production, as well as directed. This was my first directing experience with an ensemble. This, for me, was a pivotal experience which led to a lifetime of leading ensembles, musical and theatrical, one-woman shows and play writing.

It would be another 15 years before I knew anything about non-profits, funding, capital campaigns and buildings. I didn't know what we had. I couldn't have imagined how hard Reid worked to keep the Valley Studio alive. Over the years, my experience at the mime studio informed my life-long performance work in singing, film, and theatre.

Laurie Carley, Why Can't Mimes Sing?

I Wanted to Get the Movement Training

Marty Schwartz

I went to the Valley Studio because as an actor, I wanted to get the movement training I didn't get in college. We had so many great teachers come through the Valley Studio, like Hovey & Judy Burgess, Mamako Yoneyama, Carlo Mazzone Clementi, and William Burdick. Each teacher approached the work in different ways, but it was working with Reid that really turned me on. I liked the fact that Reid got us on our feet.

Reid would very often say to us, "When you learn something, you've got to get up there and either teach it or perform it." That was just the way he worked. So after we'd take a workshop with another teacher, he'd announce, "OK, you're going to work this afternoon, and then we'll come back tonight and have a Sharing. Each of you is going to come up with a sketch."

So we would work, we'd create some sketches and in the evening get up in front of each other and show them. This meant that we were constantly composing sketches, constantly improvising ideas. So we were up on our feet in front of the other students performing all the time. That was the work that resonated with me. It was good stuff, too. The work was always meaty and interesting. All of us would work very hard to use what we'd just learned. For me, this was a great way to grow as an artist. I guess Reid thought that using the new material would help cement the work into our brains and our psyches.

Joe Daly and Marty Schwartz, Aiding the Fallen

Discovering the Mask

Rosalie Jones

The Valley Studio! Such a rush of images, thoughts, implications rise up when thinking about that place and time. I cannot now recall how I came to know about Valley Studio, but my decision to study there was compelled by a curiosity, even a fascination about 'mime' and the need to expand the possibilities of the creative and performance work.

I had studied modern dance at the University of Utah, earning a master's degree, which included very useable approaches to the teaching of dance and choreography along with the then-popular techniques of Merce Cunningham and a strong dose of Alwin Nikolais. A master's thesis and production was accepted in 1966. To my astonishment, I was called to the Institute of American Indian Arts immediately after graduation, to be hired as the choreographer for an ambitious production titled "Sipapu: A Drama of Authentic Dance and Chants of Indian America" to be performed that fall in Washington, DC. All progressed well, the production took place, and I was asked to teach the following two years at IAIA. Another good fortune ensued – a scholarship to Julliard School (Dance) in New York City, followed by a year spent teaching at Flandreau and Wahpeton Indian Schools in the Dakotas. As I am of mixed blood native ancestry, it was a valuable and honorable apprenticeship of working with native peoples of the northern tribes on a teaching level and as a choreographer of student creative work. I am grateful for those experiences and the solid development of innovative native performance made possible at that time. But, by the early

1970's, I was beginning to find the materials open to me via the conventional modern dance idiom to be wearing thin. Perhaps life was wearing thin. Definitely, the creative well was in danger of running dry.

Enter: the Valley Studio! I applied as an apprentice and was accepted through 1973-74. I am sure there was a summer session or two included in the overall experience, during which I taught modern dance classes. It has always been my proclivity to save programs, newspaper announcements, photos and videos when possible, to keep a running record of my professional work. With some digging, I found an article from the Milwaukee Journal dated August, 1974, with an article titled "Indian Lore Set in Dance". That was the time in which we were living – anything "Indian" must be "lore". Gratefully, we now have more astute scholars and reporters who have taken on more appropriate terminology. But there was the article, noting that a 'Showcase' would be presented by the Wisconsin Mime Company; company members were John Aden, Terry Kerr, Kay Dubie Potter, E. Reid Gilbert. And also on the program would be a piece called "The Dispossessed" by Rosalie Jones. Admission $1.50. Reflecting on that event gives me a way to talk about The Valley Studio.

"The Dispossessed" was the one major new work I created at The Valley Studio. The work was probably not especially important to the world of mime, but for me it was significant. After years of working from the oral traditions of various northern tribes or from other peoples' writing, I was finally able to trust my own ideas and my ability to create something new, entirely from my own intuition and experiences both vicarious and real as a native woman living in contemporary times. From a program note, a synopsis of the work reads, "...the life of a young Indian woman in the boarding school, the problems encountered in the urban world and the freedom and identity finally realized by remembering her roots". This dance-mime was performed several times over the next few years. After one performance to a mostly native audience, an elderly woman spoke to me after everyone else had left. "Was that your vision?" she said gently. I was stunned. My take-away was that she had called to my attention that performance could indeed be a 'vision'; that is, a vehicle for conveying an intuition or personal revelation to other people. If I had not been given the performance tools to create "The Dispossessed", I would never have been in a place to hear these words from this Elder.

How was it possible that I came to trust myself to create this performance? I feel now that *humanity* and *creative integrity* were at the center of the work being done at The Valley Studio. Never before had I experienced a communal living situation as we had at the Studio. The apprentices and faculty lived together over months in the same complex of buildings, eating the same meals together, washing those same dishes (with assistance from Hobart!). We played together, solved our mutual problems with mutual consent, shared the discipline of regular classes in the schoolhouse, worked out creative ideas in groups, rehearsed and performed as scheduled or sometimes, impromptu! Every person there contributed an organic piece to the life of the whole. Yes, there were definitely the individual flights; personal creativity lie at the heart of it all. At this moment, I can recall being in the mime class taught by Reid, breathing deeply, warmed in sweat and the challenge of the moment. I would never master the backward "descent to the grave'! We were given a solid foundation in the art of mime and the art of mask. Coming from the 'classical' modern dance idioms, mime gave a broader field of theatricality. But it was the possibilities of the Mask that gave me the tipping point for new creative directions.

It would take more experimentation, but I finally realized that here was the key to enacting the ancient tribal stories within the native oral tradition. So many of those stories involve personages non-earthly but spiritually alive and active within our physical realm. How to depict these beings? Through 'masking' and the Mask! Now I found I could 'become' the trickster, the animals who move around us or in us, the figures of myth and the very elements of earth, fire, water, air and more. The use of the Mask opened up to interpretation, not only the oral tradition but it opened up (for me) the interpretation of the individual person. I had moved on beyond movement into the psyche, more able to explore its inner workings both internal and external.

After leaving the Valley Studio, I would teach at Mt. Scenario College in Ladysmith, Wisconsin for three years. Another good fortune brought Barry Lynn, my original mentor, to Ladysmith to live and create the Chalice Stream studio with partner Michael Doran. It was there that I began to develop dance-dramas based on oral traditions, the first being "Tales of Old Man" which utilized a masked figure as the interpretation of the Blackfeet trickster Napi. "'Tales" was followed by "The Spirit Woman", a short one-woman masked dance with text and two masks. Finally, "Wolf: A Transformation" used three masks – wolf, novice shaman and elder shaman. I consider "Wolf" to be the break-through choreography into a genre now called 'native modern dance'.

Somewhere along the way, I ran across a comment attributed to E. Reid Gilbert in which he said of my apprenticeship and teaching at Valley Studio, 'she didn't do much'. Granted, my presence and work there probably did not contribute as much as it should have. What I received in turn, however, in training and performing and living experience, set me on a unique path. The only thing I can say in my defense is that, at age thirty-two, I was still developing both personally and creatively.

In 1978 I took the ultimate step to leave the teaching position at Mt. Scenario and become a professional choreographer/performer in earnest, performing "The Spirit Woman" for 80 straight days in the summer circuit known as the Stand Rock Indian Ceremonial, Wisconsin Dells. That was the year the Boy Scouts of America relinquished control of the 'Ceremonial' to the Winnebago Nation – another step forward in restoring the sovereignty of native peoples. And it was there in 1980 that I incorporated my own company, Daystar: An American Indian Theatre, later to be named Classical Dance Drama of Indian America and finally Daystar: Contemporary Dance-Drama of Indian America. I would return to teaching, but choreography and production remained the core of Daystar: being inspired by the richness of the oral traditions of North America – the Lakota, Eastern Cherokee, Anishinaabe (Ojibway), California Maidu, the Northwest Coast, Metis and of course Blackfeet. Almost all these dance-dramas use mask in some indispensable way. Such identification is so important to me now that I prefer to be addressed as *Daystar* when teaching or choreographing.

Now, after all these years, I can say THANK YOU, REID GILBERT for the realization of *your* vision in creating the amazing place that was called "The Valley Studio".

Daystar/Rosalie M. Jones

Daystar's career spans forty-six years, during which time she taught throughout the United States and Canada to encourage and promote the development of Indigenous talent in the performing arts. Born on the Blackfeet Reservation in Montana, Daystar/Rosalie Jones carries Little Shell Chippewa ancestry through her mother's lineage. She holds a Masters Degree in Dance from the University of Utah and studied at the Juilliard School in New York City under Jose Limon. She studied mime with E. Reid Gilbert and modern with Jose Limon, Hanya Holm and Barry Lynn, whom she considers her primary 'mentor'. In 1980 she founded Daystar: Contemporary Dance Drama of Indian America, touring the United States, Canada, Ireland, Finland, Bulgaria, and Turkey. Daystar has choreographed over 30 works including *Tales of Old Man* (Blackfeet), *Sacred Woman, Sacred Earth* (Lakota), *Wolf: A Transformation* (Anishinaabe), *The Corn Mother* (Eastern Cherokee), *Prayer of the First Dancer, Allegory of the Cranes* and the scripted dance-dramas *No Home but the Heart* and *Legacy of the Dream.*

In 1997 Rosalie Jones was the first of native ancestry to receive the prestigious two-year NEA Choreographer's Fellowship; the Daystar Archive was created in 2004 at University of California-Riverside to mark a formal recognition of her work as a 'pioneer' of native modern dance. Jones is a published author, notably: *No Home But The Heart: An Assembly of Memories, Keepers of the Morning Star: An Anthology of Native Women's Theater,* UCLA, 2003; *Inventing Native Modern Dance: A Tough Trip through Paradise,* Native American Performance and Representation, U of Arizona Press, 2009. Rosalie

Jones continues to teach the courses she developed (dance, music, mime/mask, storytelling and dance production} for the Indigenous Performance program at Trent University, Ontario, Canada.

RAA Daystar

Rosalie and the three masks

Oh! I Mean It Was Classic

Patrick Sciarratta

I guess the first time I got there was 1977. So '77 and '78 were my big years at the Valley Studio. In 1977 was the first time I met Carlo Mazzone-Clementi.

Oh! I mean it was classic! It was my first time in Wisconsin. Here I am in Wisconsin, and I'm walking through the high grass alone in the afternoon, and I tripped over him! There he was lying in the tall grass completely drunk. And so I said, "Oh my God, I'm so sorry!" So as I'm stumbling over his body just lying there he said, "I am Carlo Mazzone-Clementi. It's OK. It's OK. Pardon me. I am Italian. I must have fermented grape in my body on a regular basis."

That was the first thing Carlo Mazzone-Clementi ever said to me! I just fell in love with him. What a memorable line that was.

Then he started working with me, and I asked him if he could help me with the commedia dell' arte because I had started working on it with the *I Colombiaoni* Italian clown family. I had travelled with them through Europe. They taught me how to juggle. They taught me acrobatics. They taught me a lot of stuff that I shared with Bond Street (Bond Street Theater Coalition) after that, because that was the training they really needed.

So Carlo took me under his wing. He started teaching me some commedia. He was a commedia genius, especially his Pulcinella and his Arlechino. He could create such wonderful characters. So he took me through a couple of rehearsals. He was being very formal: everything in Italian. I said, "You know, I just don't get this." He said, "Well, one thing you must learn about the commedia is that you must learn to fail magnificently." That would be another line that would carry me throughout the rest of my life, inside and outside of theater.

I kept telling him that I really didn't understand what he meant. I told him that this was all jargon, and I wasn't getting it. So the next day I come to rehearsal, and we're in the studio, and the studio is filled with people. Reid was there. All these other students were there. Friends from around the studio were there. I looked around and thought, "Obviously Carlo has told me the wrong place. We must be rehearsing somewhere else because these people are here to see a performance of some sort." So I go backstage and there is Carlo, and he is in full costume. And it dawns on me that he has put this all together so I could fail magnificently.

So I get out on stage. I can't speak Italian. I'm playing the lover, which is a forlorn character anyway. He doesn't get any laughs. So of course Carlo was getting all of the laughs. Beyond that I was completely lost, so onstage I said, "My terrible bad fortune, my lover has left me." Now Carlo is talking to me, and I'm trying to follow his words in Italian, and I'm trying to let the audience know that I'm a good actor, which made me look like even more of a simp. And people are practically peeing in their pants. This is the very nature of commedia. It is all about one-upping your partner and getting him entangled and all this stuff. I made the perfect foil because I was so innocent!

I didn't even know what I was doing, and he was eating me for dinner. I mean, he was so funny. I was so angry at him that I didn't find any of it funny, and I'm sure that really played into the characters too because the lovers were Patrician and they never knew that their servants were making fun of them. It was tremendously successful. People came up to me afterwards and said, "You just looked like so much of a freakin' idiot. That was so funny!" It wasn't like I was acting, or anything. But I did experience what "failing magnificently" was all about. Carlo was really giving it his all. Here I was going down the tubes while a master was racing around me like a top. Simply amazing.

So Carlo Mazzone-Clementi was a real factor in my life after that because anytime I spoke to him, he seemed to say things that really moved me in new directions: directions I did not know how to move before. So it was really great learning from a master many of those skills: comic timing and irony and the clever twists. I learned all of these things under his tutelage.

Another memory I have was walking through the woods with about four or five guys and Reid. Reid wanted to show us how to shuck corn. He told us that the best corn comes right off the stalk and you husk it and you run and throw it into hot water immediately so that there is like ten minutes between picking it off the plant and putting it into the water.

So we're walking around and we come to a cornfield and Reid says, "Let's take some. The farmer will never know it." So we take three or four ears each and we're holding them and I'm feeling very guilty, because I'm not a thief, yet I've taken some other guy's corn. I'm not feeling good about it. But we're following Reid Gilbert, right?

So we get to this house in the middle of nowhere and Reid says, "Let's go inside. I want to show you what a country house looks like." But I said, "We can't just go into someone's house." To which Reid replies, "No, nobody locks their doors here. Don't worry about it. We'll be in and out in a minute. I know this guy. He's not home. I want to show you what it looks like." Then I say, "Well, back in New York we call this 'breaking and entering'." And everyone kind of laughs nervously.

So we get inside and I'm still thinking this is not right. We're inside looking at somebody's house. So I say, "We gotta get out of here. I'm from Brooklyn. This is frowned upon in Brooklyn." At this point Reid says, "Don't worry. That's my cornfield and this is my house." Then we put the corn down on the table and he says that he's having a party that night. We had picked the corn for his party! That's all it was! So we didn't actually commit any crimes, we'd just helped him out by picking the corn.

BIO

Patrick Sciarratta was the executive director of FRIENDSHIP AMBASSADORS FOUNDATION from 1993 through 2015. There his focus was utilizing the ability he had amassed in physical theatre (at the Valley Studio and elsewhere) as well as the networking those opportunities enabled, to make FAF a center for peace and development through the exchange of artistic ideas and concepts. His work for more then twenty years at the foundation promoted the idea that the arts, particularly the nonverbal ones, brought people together in a common shared human experience that could be translated into diplomatic cooperation.

At the United Nations, Patrick holds delegate status through his role as Special Adviser, Permanent Mission of Sao Tome and Principe. He co-created and directed the premiere, idea leadership program for youth and the annual calendar at the U.N. Headquarters in New York since 2003, called the annual Youth Assembly at the United Nations (YA). The YA focused youth leaders on placing increased efforts toward the realization Of the UN's Global Development Agenda. Each of these programs at the UN began with and included the arts as a transformer and agent of change. He is co-editor of the *NGO Reporter,* disseminated by the UN to nearly 5000 NGOs worldwide. He has regularly served on its UN Department of Public Information (DPI) Conference Planning Committee for the past DPI NGO Conferences, he has held the position of Conference Treasurer. Under his leadership, the UN held the 2015 NGO Conference at the United Nations, with the endorsement and cooperation of four Member States at the UN, as partners for the 70th anniversary events. Patrick's personal interest in these conferences is on the empowerment of civil society and cultural exchange he is able to engender during these large scale projects.

Mr Sciarratta has worked with governments and members of the travel and culture industries to create cultural tourism products that contribute to locally-managed sustainable development. Patrick has led the foundation by focusing on the need for cultural exchange to create deep and lasting global relationships that promote mutual understanding and global cooperation. Between 2010 and 2014, he has been invited to address events in China several times, as well as in Jordan, Morocco, Albania, throughout the USA and elsewhere throughout the world. Patrick sits on the boards of the Congress of NGOs at the UN (CoNGO) and the Bond Street Theatre.

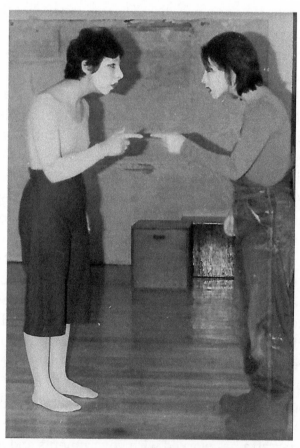

Julie B. Oak and Ann Fluckiger, Is That You?

Cars at the Valley Studio

Tarn Magnuson

We were billeted in the Wyoming Valley, south of Spring Green and miles and miles from Madison. During the day, mime and ballet and other assorted movement classes filled up our time. But come the weekend it was vehicular transportation that occupied our minds. Who had a car or truck? Was it gassed up? And could they be convinced a trip to Madison was the ideal way to spend a Saturday? I have many memories of cars from my Studio days. There was the Studio touring bus, admittedly not a car, but the best way to transport the most people (the bus, alas, lost to politics). There was Doobie Potter's vintage 50's convertible (Chevy or Olds? I can't recall), which was perfect for a prom queen candidate making an entrance up the long driveway to the Valley Studio (that was the year the dining room toaster was crowned as the winner and the three best dressed students at the prom ceremony wore nothing at all, to Miss Sally's surprise). There was Meg Partridge's VW mini-bus, which spent most weekends fixed in place while Meg stripped and rebuilt its engine (carefully following the official VW manual). There was Robyn Ander's car, with which she made demon-speed runs to Iowa (usually on her own). And there was Joe Daly's step-van (better for transporting boxes than people, brought to the Studio by Karen Flaherty and sold to Joe).

Personally, there are three vehicular memories which stand out the most:

My coldest memory is of a snowy winter night's drive I took through the Wisconsin countryside, in a car with no glass for the backseat, driver-side window (which is where I was sitting). Not that seat location really mattered, as the car had no heat what-so-ever. But I was the one dealing with the driving snow. We were also being followed by car lights, which our driver was sure belonged to a state police cruiser. He needed to make a right turn, but the car had no right turn signal, only a left. Fearful of getting a ticket, and deaf to our pleas that he chance the turn with a hand signal, so we could seek the warmth and shelter of our final destination, the driver chose to make three mile-long country road lefts to achieve the desired right. I do not believe the driver, whose identity is lost in the mists of time, ever had another passenger for the remainder of the winter.

My most expensive memory is of the night Jonathan was arrested. He was on the way back from Madison, driving through Black Earth, made famous by its speed trap. Let's admit it, more than likely, Jonathan was speeding. But that's where his trouble just began. For, after being pulled over by the fine-happy police, he aroused their suspicions when he tried to change places with front-seat passenger Craig Silvey. Jonathan, it turns out, did not possess a valid driver's license. This meant the very youthful looking mime had no proof of age. So, erring on the side of caution, he was sent back to Madison and their juvenile detention facility. The ticketed car was allowed to continue on to the Wyoming Valley. The Studio became a blaze of lights as one and all were roused from sleep in an effort to raise the money to bail out Jonathan. This, at a time when the minimum wage was $1.60 an hour, and most of the students were church-mouse poor. From out of nowhere, John Aden popped up wearing a "Free Jonathan" button. (It might have been an altered "Free John Sinclaire" button.) Eventually, we reached the bottom of our pockets and sprang Jonathan from jail.

My favorite car memory is when I joined John and Doobie as guest artists for a week at Northland College, in Ashland, Wisconsin. This town lay to the far north, on the shore of Lake Superior. It was divided in half by a small river, over which ran a solitary bridge. Toward the end of our week, we decided to hit the town for an evening of wining and dining, and capped the night off with a bad movie. Driving back to our dorm rooms at Northland, we searched in vain for the lone bridge across the river. We knew it had to be there. John suffered the backseat driving of Doobie and myself (well, mostly Doobie) for as long as he could and then made a command decision. He took what he thought was the correct left turn, only, after a slight bump and a change in road conditions, to discover it was an abandoned and unused driveway. Suddenly, there we were, cruising through the back yards of an Ashland neighborhood, dodging small bushes, flower beds and swing sets. Doobie helped out by cracking up in gleeful laughter. And even while searching for a way out, John was swearing me to secrecy. No one back at the Studio was to know this had ever happened. (I believe the thirty-year rule applies in this matter.) Eventually, we found a real road again, and the bridge, and our beds for the night. All in all, a most satisfying road trip.

   Tarn

Addendum

It seems that Valley Studio vehicles (not always just automobiles) remain in the memory bank of several of the VS people.

One of course was the retired hearse, as noted in Grant Bashore's story.

An old school bus was used for major tours, traveling all the way from North Dakota to Georgia and several venues in between. One stop was in North Carolina, where we visited my Dad and stepmother. The old bus was a lemon and quite often went on strike in most perplexing spots.

Only a few miles from my Dad's the bus stalled and all its lights went out on a two lane rural road (Old Hollow Road). Of course, everything that would occur at the studio or on tour would be considered as a lazzo (comic bit) in a commedia del arte scene, no matter how compromised the situation would be. The guys in the bus emerged (just before midnight) and with a great sense of comedy and celebration began pushing the bus, while Joe Daly was trying to start it. I said, "Boys, cut out the comedy routine and push this bus into a yard. A local factory lets out its second shift of workers at midnight, and they fly down this road. They won't be able to see you in time to stop." They did follow my instructions, with no further difficulty except for me to explain to the startled neighbors what was happening and to ask permission of them to leave the bus there until the next day to get it fixed. Fortunately Dad lived close by and everyone had a place to sleep, including the basement. While Doobie was doing the laundry for everyone, we did get the bus started.

The bus was later sold to the gubernatorial campaign for Lee Dreyfus. I served on his committee to represent the arts. Dreyfus did not get the endorsement of the Republican Convention , even though he was running as a republican. It seems that they considered him a republicrat. When his campaign committee met in Stevens Point to commiserate over the lack of funds and no political endorsement, we were asked to provide some plan to continue the campaign. Knowing what a wonderful public speaker Lee was, I said, "What Lee needs is a whistle-stop train."

Lowell Jackson said, "Reid you artists are all alike. We have a real problem here and you suggest a daydream. A whistle-stop train? Get practical! We can't even afford a school bus."

"Well I have a school bus which has a metal platform at the back even with a steel railing. You could make a campaign stop in a town and let Lee emerge out the back door to make his speech. It also has a wooden platform on the top where we store our sets and props while on tour. You could put a little high school oompah band on top to provide music to announce your arrival as you roll into the town square."

That plan was adopted. Dreyfus won the election and later donated the bus to a Boy Scout ranch in New Mexico.

Period Dance Group: Janis Wykoff, Joe Daly, Kate Lunga, Tarn Magnuson, Adrienne Gilbert, Joe Long, Doobie Potter, and Dennis Richards

Reid Called Out My Name

Joe Daly

Reid called out my name as I stepped two-by – two scaled rustic wood beam-nosed steps that led to the upper dorms and dining hall. I slowed my gait on the large pebbled upper walkway to let him catch up.

"You still have your rifle?"

Tentatively I answered, "Yeah." I slowed even more mid-answer, my mind derailed from anticipation of dinner. Was I too late for the main course?

"Why?" I asked, wondering if my earlier disclosure was a mistake. I kept it with me when I began my second year of apprenticeship to his company.

"Two geese are snagged up in a barbed-wire fence at a friend's farm across the valley. They've offered them for our school to have for Thanksgiving if we'll get them cleared before they're dead."

We reached the end of the loose and rattling pebble walk, entered the dining hall together and my thoughts lurched from blank stunned wonder at being asked about my simple gun to serious doubt about gathering sufficient resolve to actually fire it after several years of quiet safekeeping and occasional cleaning.

After one of his six month tours of sea duty my father came home and gave matching single action .22 gauge rifles to me and my brother Dave when I was eleven years old and he was ten. I learned to shoot with target practice but hunted with it only very few times on our Michigan farm. I'd only kept it with me when I traveled to study as a way to prevent mischief, so with no use for it in mind I quietly kept it mostly concealed from the other apprentices.

Actually shooting the geese turned out to be less stressful than anticipated. They were in a bad way and growing weaker there at the edge of a frozen pond and the idea of rescue didn't make sense. I feared not only their natural mean demeanor but also the too-new ice along the pond edges which would probably crack under my weight if I were struggling with live and defensive birds. Even stressed they would doubtless snap at my fingers. Both of these factors would easily dissuade anyone from attempting to confront the dilemma completely hands-on. And so it was obvious they needed to be killed, and Reid was correct to suggest my gun for the job.

By the time the birds were in the oven they had been dutifully and imaginatively utilized. The feathers were made into cushions by a few other students in the apprentice program, and though my duties as one of several cooks implied a share of distasteful butchery, many other willing hands pitched in with the messy jobs of gutting, blood draining, plucking, and cleaning. All was done quite efficiently but with a sober tone. No one liked doing it, but each consent implied a further duty until the meal we planned was had.

The meal was very good and the unusual flavors were enjoyed by most of us, but no matter how nourishing and tasty, I knew I had no interest in repeating the experience of putting a bullet through any animal's head and cutting it apart to remove innards and drain blood.

My father's words on the subject of being in charge combined with this experience to trip in me a new resolve that changed my life.

And that's how I became a vegetarian.

Of course it was not a difficult decision while among so many staunch vegetarians there.

In more than one way and on more than one occasion from the time I was a little boy my father told me "If you are in a position of leadership never ask someone to do something you are unwilling to do yourself". I'm sure his intention was to share a distilled response to countless encounters with bad leadership he'd experienced in the

Navy, but for me the idea presented a surgical method and impulse for self-examination which fell (and still fall) along these lines:

What is this grand and advantageous system of specializations in society? I can raise potatoes well while you make excellent furniture, and we each contribute to more and better overall yields for the sum of our efforts if we let each other focus, but if one of us devolves this cooperation to spin unsavory yet imperative tasks as beneath anyone's dignity, if ever I feel cleaning the toilet is the job others ought to mind so I may never, we've regressed to virtual slavery once more.

If I find myself unwilling to butcher an animal for food I truly have no business waiting for others to do it, I truly should eat no meat.

And so that's why I stopped.

DALY BIO

Joe Daly works as a stagehand in New York City at The Metropolitan Opera and NBC and has steadily served as a carpenter for Saturday Night Live for 27 years. He also regularly teaches dance in New York and on occasion in Mumbai.

Kathak Dance, Gina Lalli

I Will Never Forget

Betsy Folsom

I will never forget the first time I drove onto the long, curving gravel drive and saw the magical place that was to become my home for the next two years or so – the school house on the right, the lush green carpeted hill leading to the farm house, and behind it the dining room and dorms all under the protection of the woods behind. This pastoral scene became the background on which a group of young, idealistic theatre geeks lived, breathed, learned, practiced, critiqued, and encouraged each other in not only the art of mime, but the art of living.

No matter what hour of the day or night, almost every inch of those grounds and/or buildings were filled with joyous laughter, serious discussions, struggles to put ideas into movement and final rehearsals. Our valiant leader, Dr. E. Reid Gilbert, had us up, dressed and in a yoga warm-up at 6:30 am each day, followed by breakfast and morning classes. Then we had a break before lunch, afternoon classes, a break before dinner and rehearsals or discussions in the evenings.

During the year, we studied mime technique and composition, ballet, modern dance, juggling, clowning, etc. In the summer we had amazing people from all over the world as special instructors in arts including: Japanese mime, Commedia del Arte, the Alexander technique. On the weekends all year round we hosted high school theatre students and their teachers, to share in the experience of 24/7 creativity. One summer we hosted an international mime convention and toured a caravan of performers from Spring Green through Madison to Milwaukee.

I grew up at the studio. I entered the summer of my college graduation, a kid with dreams, and an ego-centric view of the world. I left a few years later having learned how to live, share, work, struggle and succeed as a community of people to start my own life.

Indoor landscaping

Valley Whispers and Reflections
Deborah LaFond

How to begin? I guess by saying hello to all! Have felt your presence but have also so missed you all! Joined this dance-call for stories way near the end, but here goes!

Early 1970's, somehow I stumbled into a mime class hosted at the University of Wisconsin – Milwaukee by Barbara Leigh. As a young female, former free school student, auto mechanic, factory worker, taking African dance, had co-created a feminist theater troupe (Luna Rythms), I recall feeling something open in Barbara's mime class. Barbara Leigh guided us on a meditation before moving... I remember seeing in my mind's eye a path through trees... This vision has stayed with me my whole life and I take it very seriously. Not so interested in speaking at that time in my life... but had much rumbling in me..., Barbara said, well if you like this, there is a Mime school up north in Wisconsin. I grew more curious, drove up to Spring Green. Wisconsin with my mom, all of 18-19 years of age.

Greeted by lovely Nina (Roger and family) who worked the front office, lived down the road, we were welcomed and cared for daily. From a working class, civil rights activist, feminist family from Milwaukee and Madison, I for one did not think I could afford to come, but a way was found. As lunch cook and dorm painter/cleaner, renovation and floor sander, I was invited to work and study and join the crazy cook crew, Hi John, Betsy, Janis, Joe, Midnight and all! The kitchen, good food, and dining room, as Reid had intended, was a critical part of the school and community gathering space, especially in the winters when access to whatever went on in the Teepee and elsewhere, was not as accessible.

Living together as a zany, creative artist community nestled within the incredible beautiful meandering streams, rivers, hills, rich farmland, and ancestral land of Wisconsin with neighbors working on the land and other artists in the community, many walks, visiting regularly — a woman weaver down the road, the cheese factory the other way... Taliesin and Frank Lloyd Wright near by, knowing the visionary apprentice connection to these two spaces... for me, this was exploratory space, seemingly, open to all who came. Remember, how we were a strange lot when descending on the small town local bar to dance and party but little by little, it seemed we were at least tolerated there as some sort of spectacle while we explored moving in other community spaces?

Recalling how a donor of land, Nina, Reid and company held and facilitated. Reid Gilbert, founder, visionary, artist who shared his very down to earth sensibility, love of land, Appalachia wisdom, humor — shared his disciplined mime and Japanese Noh training/philosophy, as he stomped next to our ears in daily morning meditations to help us consider how this practice must carry into our daily lives, in stillness and in chaos. Working apprentice philosophy meant physical/emotional labor, in addition to the artistic work and practice and very much influenced as it engendered stronger bonds and deeper artistic work. Respecting the ground we worked on every day, our daily ritual of cleaning the floor before we began our mime work was such a humbling ritual that seemed to influence our creativity, grounded us and seemed to help us unfetter from whatever worlds we came from. How else would we agree to dive off roofs into the arms of students catching us below in our "trust exercises" in circus techniques class?

As apprentice, for me, this was not polished production/performance path space but an integrated, exploratory approach to art, earth, spirit, an embodied community through the work of mime, movement, dance, masks, comedia drawing from both national and international art scenes, connected through love of play, ecstatic expression of movement/spirit and storytelling. This storytelling however, expressed through non-verbal (though not strictly) allowed for a greater sense of witness and respect for both seen and unseen, a form and practice I had never imagined could BE a way of life... Though traversing to Paris to continue to study, not recognizing this connection in other mime spaces made it difficult for me to continue that path though other ways opened up. To know oneself as mover and to be known as mover continues to sustain and bring joy throughout the many trials of my life and I hope for yours as well!

Remember those "intelligent moments" (Tom L. used to say) during silent witnessing of two people (or more) at the table, inter- actions waiting for something improvisational to emerge (Hi Susan, Karen and all)? From corporeal mime (Tom Leabhart), so many mime approaches, Native American and modern dance(Rosalie and others), the Comedia dell'Arte group from Italy, the Bharata Natyam, ballet, circus techniques, to Body Wisdom classes and more, all of these teachers shared their hearts and art with us. A new language, a possibility of creating spirit and connection across the globe – remains to this day for me and guides my instincts – when I listen...

Did you all have the sense of being part of and witnessed by the natural world surrounding us – a connection we were encouraged to experience and value? Posing on the rocks with photographers? Where did those pictures go I wonder? "Go to the woods, mind the ticks in the pine groves, make a mask from nature, feel the face of others, feel the mask, move with the mask." In our mask making class held in the studio with the costume shop, I will never forget Reid sending us outdoors to find natural artifacts to create a mask – how affirming Reid was when I came back with a dried manure "cow pie" I found to create a mask from. Reid so respected my choice. Remember the night when Reid came through the dorms to the kitchen, with his hair standing up, so surprised and alert to the bobcat call he heard while walking the trail at night?

As a child in a family of 8, I always moved and danced to music.

Not sure I saw myself as creator at that time, more of a "seeker", as Reid would say. At the studio, very unique emerging identity was growing– simple and complex but somehow untouchable to the forces of ill... To know you are nature and no matter what, you know your embodied and have internal connection with land and movement, as if nothing else needed to matter... this internal seeing and wanting to affirm this for others seemed to be wholly part of the mission of the Valley Studio.

For me, there was witness with so little judgement, didn't even have to speak about judgement, everyone seemed to know this was an organic sacred space, not that we didn't judge ourselves but for me, it was more play—though some knew more about themselves as movers and creators, co-creators, than others.

How to bring this back into my life when considering leaving the studio? I recall inviting folks to a meeting in my room in the dorm to discuss political theater. Hazel and Alice music playing in the background, Reid stopped by, maybe a bit fearful, inquisitive, but liked the music, after conversation, then showed respect to my questions, Reid wrote a poem about our interaction there. "While cities burn..." Might anyone have that poem? I'm sure I have it somewhere. Tom Leabhart and Alexander instructors, hearing my critiques and concerns, came to the kitchen to try out how Alexander Technique could be applied to kitchen work as well as singing and movement!

Sharing this work with community, working with young children in the summer studio workshops and in Wisconsin schools, to open up some carcerative education spaces and encourage young folks to create this sense of embodiment and creativity was an extremely happy culmination of our work at the studio (Wisconsin schools – Thank you all, Reid, Kay Doobie Potter, John Aden , Joe Long, others).

For me, still learning to listen, find face, voice, balance, dare I say, the artist in me, but mostly meaning and action that respects indigeneity and our planetary home... Each day I gaze upon the "The Song of the Lark" as expressed by Jules Breton in the painting (Le

Chant De L'Alouette, 1884). I take this into my work and movement with me and I associate this painting with my Valley Studio-Spring Green experience throughout my persistent performances and attempts to create/facilitate community, free, inquiring, intellectual spaces as librarian and educator. I am ever so grateful for this Valley Studio, Spring Green home and community.

Reid Gilbert and Doobie Potter, Pierot Wooing the Goddess

How I First Heard of the Valley Studio

Michael Shimkus

In 1974 I was working at Good Karma Café, a vegetarian restaurant/performance space/"head shop"/craft store on State Street in Madison, Wisconsin. Many storied and legendary artists were playing at this venue. Willie Dixon, Charles Mingus, Stanley Turentine, John Fahey, Vassar Clemens, etc. Workshops of various types were also offered at Good Karma. Tai Chi, aromatherapy, etc. If one worked at the "collective," one could attend these workshops free of charge.

Well, it so happened that a man named David Brennan was doing a massage workshop there. I took the workshop, and in the course of it, found out that David was enrolled in a small "mime" school thirty-eight miles west of Madison called the Valley Studio. He was very enthusiastic about his experience there and this piqued my curiosity. As a consequence, well, "Lo and behold," I believe it was in August of '74 that the entire Mime Troupe of the aforementioned Valley Studio had a performance at the Good Karma Café. Reid Gilbert, John Aden, Terry Kerr and Kay Doobie Potter did a performance of Pierrot. It was such a charming experience! After the performance, David Brennan introduced me to everyone and they all said, "Oh, come and enroll in the school. You'll love it!" I was smitten. They invited me for a weekend to see what the place and space were all about. I remember partying with Terry Kerr and Ted Lange (a friend of the Valley Studio). I enrolled the following January in 1975.

#2 – My most vivid memories

I have many vivid and wonderful memories of the Valley Studio. During my first semester, there was an account imbalance and we were asked to fast one day per week in order to lessen the food bill. I think later on we hunted and killed a deer or two in order to eat them. I remember some people had a difficult time with this...

One thing I remember vividly is the physical beauty of the land: the hills across from the dorms, and the hills straight past the open fields...these fields would sometimes have 50...100...200 deer in them. It was wonderful to see the seasons change there... the autumn was spectacular...the winter magical. Spring was miraculous and summer was a total blast. Fecundity spiraled around everyone and everything. A Dionysian, riotous symphony of life...

I remember doing a ritualistic pre-class warm-up: going through the positions; sitting on haunches, knees tucked under; then one leg out, foot flat and the other leg still tucked under, change legs, then both feet flat, knees bent, butt down. Then the "coup de grace": crouched down, bearing weight on one leg; the other leg is CROSSED atop the thigh of the crouched weight-bearing leg, the weight-bearing leg alternates back and forth between bearing weight on ball of foot (heel up), then foot flat (heel down), back and forth, at least three times, then one stood back up, rising up from the now very tired weight-bearing leg. Then lying down (in the sun if it was out), and waiting for Reid Gilbert to start the class.

There were the times when we would do all the ritual warm-ups and be lying down focusing and Reid would come in and announce that the whole class was to go back to the room and change into clothes appropriate for hiking! We would all change clothes and Reid would lead us on a very challenging hike...as 19-20 year-olds we were indeed challenged. It was always exhilarating when this happened (though rare). Reid knew the land as well as anyone. He would identify plants and trees along the way.

I remember that Doc Connor (I believe this was the name of a physician who financed the Valley Studio) owned some land near the Valley Studio. On his property there was an abandoned house there, as well as an abandoned apple orchard. Reid had us pick apples which we brought back to Valley Studio where there was an old-fashioned cider press. In the first cylinder, the apples were perforated and cut. When full, these cylinders were moved sixteen inches and put under the press, a cylindrical turn screw that squeezed all juice out of the apples. We also found wild grapes growing in profusion. Purple-frosted, deep, deep, dark, succulent, and wild...these we also juiced and I remember all of us putting our mouths such that the juice would fall into our mouths.

I remember opening to the summer session. It was early evening. Forty or so people were doing Sufi Stick Dances. Everyone had two dowels of pine about three feet long, and this pattern emerged:

Each person would circle around the person in front of him or her and go in a circle: person A's right hand with stick connected to person B's left hand with stick. Around in a circle these two persons turned. When the pair completed one revolution, each went to the next person, and the turning action was repeated. It was truly ecstatic!

Simple and Elaborate memories...

Reid teaching Jitter Bug (the man could dance)!!

I remember the Faux Prom. Everyone was in character the whole time. John Aden's character was a coach/jock, totally-straight-up, suburban guy. He was really struggling with my "Clockwork Orange-bad boy-with-a-streak-of-violence-in-him" character. Jude Brister played a developmentally-delayed person who I just wanted to do bad things to. John Aden kept breaking it up. I remember the dancing was a lot of fun that night.... I remember Reid being above it all. I can picture Mary Galati, John Russell, Marty Schwartz, Sue Miller.

#4 Classes

I took many classes at the Valley Studio: Corporeal Mime, Zen Mime with Mamako Yoneyama, Acting Improvisation, Stage Combat, Ballet, Modern Dance, Alexander Technique, Circus Arts, Pottery, Gardening, and Mask Making.

I have to admit I found mask-making completely mysterious

and amazing. It was the act of creation personified. The first part of mask-making was applying petroleum jelly to one's face and then making a plaster cast of one's face. Thin strips of plaster gauze were wet and applied to the face.

At this point, the face was completely covered in plaster gauze, except for the openings for the nostrils to breathe. In such a state the person who applied your mask then took you for a walk. Because one was walking blindly, one had to depend completely on the partner to lead him or her.

When the mask dried, it was removed. The second stage was to pour into the mask plaster of Paris. Some people did not do this and instead used the mask as it was. I was not one of those people. When the plaster of Paris dried, one took the mold of one's face and used it as a basis in which to apply Plasticene – an oil-based clay that does not easily dry. Once applied, one could shape the clay in any shape that one wished. Then the creator applied papier mache to the plasticene, and lo and behold...one has the shape... after applying Gesso. Then came the painting of the mask, and the drilling holes: two for sight, and two for the mask to be attached to one's head. That was when the fun started.

How was it when one was smiling under the mask? Was it obvious to one and all? And what if one was frowning? Or any other primary emotion? It was magical to be introduced to masks.

#5 Chores

In late May/early June, in between the spring session and the summer session, I was part of the crew who stayed in order to work and to supplement my tuition. There was painting, grounds keeping...all manner of tasks to be accomplished. The biggest project during that gap between sessions was the tilling and planting of the garden. Now this garden was not a little garden plot. It was an extra-large, king-sized garden. I'm recollecting it to be perhaps thirty yards long by fifteen or twenty yards wide. I think the crew consisted of Reid, David Brennan, myself, and a couple of other people whom I cannot recall.

Now remember – Reid designed the garden to feed fifty people during summer sessions. There was lettuce, spinach, carrots, tomatoes, beets, corn, arugula, and more. Well, the day we chose for planting must have been the nastiest, hottest, most humid, mosquito-infested inferno of hell that had ever hit southwest Wisconsin. If you have ever planted a garden you know how maddeningly tiny the seeds are...just a little north of molecules really, and very delicate somehow...Well all of us were holding the seeds in the palm of one hand...putting them in the ground with the other hand and in between plantings, slapping the mosquitoes as fast as fast could be...to no effect did these swats have. There was an ocean full of mosquitoes in the sky that day. They did not quite blot out the sun, but I'm sure they diminished the light by a few degrees. We were all of us hollering, cursing, screaming and generally going a little crazy. At the end of the day, at twilight, our faces were all swollen to a scary degree. I thought we might have to be hospitalized it looked so gruesome. I was very proud of that garden when it bloomed and gave up its bounty.

#6 Performances

At the Valley Studio and especially in the summer, there were so many performances...So much genius on display, so much ingenuity. But my favorite performances were during the year when there were just twenty people at the school. Two performances in particular come to mind...after the autumn of '75 semester; we rented in Richland Center a small yet elegant theatre with a Proscenium Stage. The theatre was a little "faded around the edges," but quite charming. I think it could hold three hundred people. Instead of finales, we performed the piece or pieces we had worked on during the school year. The title of my piece was, "The Wizard of Wyoming Valley." It was a great adventure...

The other performance was at the University of Wisconsin, Green Bay. Here the whole school did a workshop performance. I felt so proud to be instructing other people in various techniques. After all the performers' workshops, we all went out dancing to a place that was a former bowling alley. It was huge, and had great wooden flooring. When the entirety of the Valley Studio went out dancing it was a cosmic event. It always turned into a performance act. We were *breakdancing* twenty years before anyone else had even *heard* of breakdancing! We lit up the dance floor...no, that is not true. We SCORCHED the dance floor with such wit, grace, beauty, love and joy, as to be blinding....

Commedia del Arte Performance on the Porch Stage

9 What have I been able to use since then, including current thoughts

The Valley Studio was the defining experience of my life, for it was here that I landed at 19 years old after a very tumultuous 15 years. I had no life plan and lots of energy. It was at the Valley Studio that I received guidance and revelation which made clear my life's work. This work was to write Opera and other multi-media extravaganza. But first I had to learn how to create music!

This path I am still on. I have achieved artistic success but not commercial as of yet. My other constant goal was always and will always be to get back to the Valley Studio, to be in an environment with a group of fellow creators collaborating to our hearts content

Ghosts in the Valley

Kirk Olgin

Long before Spring Green ever existed, there was only Wyoming Valley. However, Wyoming Valley remained uninhabited because the indigenous people believed that the Valley was inhabited by great spirits. Nevertheless, European settlers ignored the so-called beliefs and non-indigenous people have lived there ever since. As a reflection of the spirits, Edna Meudt wrote a poem about arriving late on horseback to a birthday party at Taliesin East only to become horrified as she watched a demented grounds keeper axe to death children as they left the ablaze home of Frank Lloyd Wright.

In addition to the stories of spirits, late, late at night various students at Valley Studio would tell about a spirit that roamed around the Valley Studio. They told the story of a woman who had lived where the Valley Studio now exists. As the story goes, a guest was to meet the woman at an agreed time; however, when the guest arrived, the woman was nowhere to be found. A tea kettle was whistling on the stove, so the guest waited thinking that she could not be far. The woman never appeared again. She was gone forever.

Years later, at Valley Studio students would complain about a woman who would appear from a different dimension. Some told stories about seeing her; others told stories about hearing her and others told about feeling her. Michael Shimkus once told me and others that he had seen a ghost. Many were skeptical but I argued that he could not have been that pale if he had made it up.

Nonetheless, it seemed unscientific, so I too remained skeptical.

And then, one summer night I decided to sleep outside—in front of the house right by the potato cellar. It was a most magnificent night filled with stars as only one who has been in Wyoming Valley knows. Lying on the ground, I felt a wonderful fullness with the earth and the galaxy above.

I was awakened by a loud buzzing sound. However, this sound came with a strong feeling that was trying to take over my being. And a struggle began. For some reason or other the buzzing and its spirit seemed nefarious. I immediately recognized it as a possession with a remarkable strong force. Suddenly to ward off what I deemed as a being, all things spiritual came to mind. I had been an altar boy in elementary school, so I began reciting the Mass in Latin. That is, everything I could remember: anything positive. Before I came to the Valley Studio, I had lived in the most sacred city in India (Vrndaban). I began reciting everything I knew in Sanskrit. It worked; the spirit disappeared. However, it was only for a while. Suddenly, with an unbelievable force it returned. I screamed out Hail Mary and the Gayatri Mantra. It dissipated to goodness knows where. I went back to the dormitory where I sat downstairs in complete consternation until sunrise. I never told this story to anyone.

One day, Michael and I were in the house and he told me that the ghost was here. I asked him where because I wanted to see it. However, Michael told me that it had gone away and amused by the incident explained that it did not like me.

Perhaps the ghost who is a woman still haunts Valley Studio or other spirits roam Wyoming Valley.

Addendum

I find Kirk's story fascinating, even though I never encountered the ghost. However one evening on a Fourth of July, I decided to get away from the hustle and bustle of the Studio. I only told Rosalie Jones, so that someone would know I was up in the pine forest, if I might have been needed for anything

As it was a full moon, I didn't bother with a flashlight. About halfway up the hill, I was suddenly startled by screaming which seemed to be emanating from a spot only a few feet away to my right. I stood my ground, even though my heart was racing like the Indy 500. I had never been frightened out of any woods, and I wasn't going to be haunted that night. as I stood stock still, though not calmly. The critter, which sounded like a woman screaming, began to move away, still screaming though making no movement sound like brushing through the undergrowth.

After gaining my composure, I hastened up to the pines. The trees were so close together that I had to push the branches aside to get through. Then I heard it again, but this time it was to my left and again began moving away but in the opposite direction toward Rush Creek.

I figured that the ungodly being, whatever it was, didn't like me, especially my presence in his domain. I wasn't about to stay and argue with the fellow, so I made my way as hastily as possible to the powerline which was cleared of any trees or underbrush. Actually that was in the direction of the first screamer, but I reckoned that if he attacked me I would be able to see what it was.

This time about halfway down the power line to the Studio I heard him again in the edge of the woods to my left.

I got back to my apartment safely and decided that I didn't need to commune with nature that particular night.

erg

Excited About the Possibilities

Thomas Ukinski

I don't remember how I first became aware of the Valley Studio. I was doing stand-up comedy in Chicago in the mid-1970s, and a friend suggested I study mime to help me relax on stage and improve my delivery. Somehow I found out that the Studio had a one-week program in the summer.

That week proved to be very challenging for me. I was a city dweller dropped into a lush natural environment. The regimen of classes was formidable. I was extremely tense and rigid in posture and not previously engaged in any kind of physical fitness activity. The classes in ballet were overwhelming. Most discomfiting of all was the incredible energy generated by so many young people. In a short while, though, I became excited by the possibilities opened up to me. Could someone in this world actually be able to live the life of an artist, a mime?

When I returned to Chicago and resumed my stand-up avocation, people commented that I seemed to have more poise, and looked fitter. That, in only a week! Until then, becoming a writer and a comedian was the focus of all of my aspirations. I was a dutiful employee of the U.S. Postal Service, an actor in community college productions, and the iconoclastic product of a degree in Philosophy from a Jesuit college. I railed at my bondage and dreamed of artistic and existential fulfillment.

I decided that whatever was happening in Chicago and in my present life would not change. I had to make the change, or, rather, change myself. I resigned from the Post Office, although the union representative said that there were "a hundred guys" waiting to take my place, and I was a fool to throw away a wonderful career with the Service. I was able to cash out my meager pension, which was enough to leave Chicago and pay the tuition and living expenses at the Studio. Somehow, without a job, I was able to survive and thrive.

It took me a long while to exchange the indomitable rhythms of city life for the tranquil flowing patterns that imbued the trees and hills of Spring Green, Wisconsin. The urge toward self-expression, the cravings of youth to make life an intense experience of wonderment, the needs for companionship and intimacy, all kept me off-balance. But there was a new sense of purpose, refined with the daily discipline of classes, which carried me forward. In ballet and jazz dance classes I was doing things with my body that would have been impossible to conceive of a few months before. Through Reid's guidance in the fundamentals of mime, I not only learned how to manipulate space, to create a wall or a glass box, or enact a ritual in a face mask, but also how to transmit a myriad of ideas and emotions with a gesture. What moved me so much was his performances as a storyteller—something I had wanted to be my whole life and had sought to become through writing and comedy.

As I and my classmates and friends, including Kirk Olgin, Steve Wasson and Mike Shimkus, became schooled in the fundamentals of mime and circus arts, we became enamored of the possibilities of silent comedy. We studied the films of Buster Keaton and Charlie Chaplin and embraced the ethos of the clown. I remember going to a performance of Jakob Dimitri, then known as "Dimitri Clown." What was amazing not only his incredible agility and musicianship, but the way he could take the most commonplace items, like the contents of an audience member's purse, and create humor and poignancy that transcended language, place and time. At one point he let a slender rubber hose fall out of his hands and had to painstakingly roll it back into his fist, only to have the hose tumble out again. The expression of his face as he engaged in this repetitive task expressed the boredom and frustration of every person consigned to drudgery.

A performance of *Noh* Theater, in which Reid participated, showed the nobility and profundity of restraint, composure and *Kitari & Kamigakari*, in which all inconsequential action is eliminated, leaving the essence of the scene.

Similar in this regard is the art of corporeal mime, introduced shortly before I left the Studio, in which the most ordinary actions are abstracted into the epitome of movement.

On one mid-term break, a number of us traveled through Mexico doing mime in villages and tourist areas. During another, Kirk and I traveled around the East Coast doing street mime in Boston, Philadelphia and Washington, DC. We would draw crowds by imitating people as they passed by. After leaving the Studio, I was hired by a theater company in Iowa for a traveling children's show. I drew upon my training to do not only singing and dancing but also slapstick. One sketch I recall devising concerned the reactions of an insectile Martian to a soda pop can that had been left behind by earthling picnickers. From there my wife and I (whom I'd met in the theater company) went on to do a two-person comedy show in schools and nightclubs in the Boston area, and on a children's television show in Providence.

Although I did not continue as a performer, and followed other paths, including my present occupation as a lawyer, I still maintain a love and appreciation for physical comedy. I was able to incorporate my training in my writing, in descriptions of actions, gestures, and expressions of face and body. I have been successful in retaining a habit of exercise that would not likely have developed without the guidance and inspiration of the Studio.

It goes without saying that the Valley Studio was an unforgettable experience that altered the course of my life. I will be forever grateful to Reid and the amazing teachers, students and staff of the Valley Studio.

This is a poem that I wrote for Reid:

The Mime

(for E. Reid Gilbert)

Tensely pliant, the leonine reeds
sliver silvered marsh with brush-stroke shadows
as he passes, pearled by dawn,
flanneled and fatigued,
his russet hair like purling grass,
his graved face raged by glimmering
while thick-backed hills mutter sunrise.
Greasepaint and silken white
blur him discarnate.
Serpentine in stagelight
he limns tenuous beings
who shape him with shudderings.
Slim striate arms
force strength upon itself.
Glyphic immobility
similizes objects,
as only the human can not-do
and be rhythmless amidst the city.
Through interstitial trees he sees
gray crowds of women
coddling the downy sun;
hears scrapings and chirrings
and whispering wraiths
and absorbs the rhythms for a storytelling dance.

*portrays

hyeroglyphic
sculpture

Mingling with the Locals
Doobie Potter

One of the fun things about being at the Valley Studio for six years was that we were constantly mingling with the locals. I don't know if Reid ever told you this story. There was a Spring Green Softball Team. The Studio was going to play a game against them. The winner of the game would get a keg of beer donated by Bob's Friendly Tavern (where some of us would mingle with the locals).

So for the game, we all had characters. Reid was the pitcher. He wore bib overalls and we called him "Country Reid." I was the coach. That was my character. I had a whistle and a clipboard and everything. We had cheerleaders in leotards and tights and whiteface. Susan Chreitzberg was one of the cheerleaders. The Spring Green Softball Team had real uniforms and cleats.

We actually practiced in the field at the Studio to get ready. We practiced the softball as well as the theater. During the game when a Spring Green player would hit a home run, the cheerleaders would go out and build an invisible wall so the runner couldn't get to home plate.

We also had halftime entertainment. We had people on unicycles, juggling, and fire juggling, all sorts of stuff. Of course the Studio team lost. Then we all went together to Bob's Friendly Tavern and drank the keg of beer. So we got it anyway.

Another time there was a local community theater in Spring Green, and they were doing a production of Born Yesterday. A couple of weeks before their production was supposed to open, the woman who was cast as Billy Dawn found out she couldn't do the play. Now I had done the part of Billy Dawn before in another production and somebody had heard I could do it, and so I stepped in and performed the role for them.

You've got to remember that the Billy Dawn character is a dumb blond, and she's pretty promiscuous. I guess I was too believable in the role because Reid said that after the show all these farmers were calling the Studio and they were wanting to meet me. (chuckles) They wanted to get to know me. We'd have to dissuade them from thinking I was like her. (laughs) I guess I played it too real, too good.

THE SELF MASK

That first summer when I went to the Studio (I don't know if it was 1970 or 1971) Reid was working on masks. My friend Carlos was in the class. Carlos was a really dark skinned black person. There were no other black people that lived in the Spring Green area back then.

We'd make these masks out of plaster bandages. Then we would do all sorts of partner exercises in the masks. One of the things we'd do was trust walks with each other. The one in the mask could breathe because there were holes for the nostrils, but they couldn't see because the plaster bandages covered your eyes, and their partner would guide them around outside.

Well, Carlos decided that he'd go on a trust walk on his own. He puts on his white plaster mask and proceeds down the dirt road in front of the Studio. Now imagine yourself coming around a curve on a dirt road in the country and seeing a black man walking down the road with a white mask on, showing no features, no eyes. This local guy driving a Jeep did just that, and he ran off the road into a ditch. It freaked him out so much! Stuff like that would happen with the locals all the time!

BIO

I use everything I learned at Valley Studio and have since I left. I just removed two touring groups from the Oklahoma Touring

Program. They were The Prime Mime Time Players with Joe Long and Craig Silvey. Also Zap! The Zany Arts Players with Joe Long and a performer I have worked with since the 80s, Rhonda Clark. This is a Commedia Troupe. I have taught theatre and Mime for 29 years for ages 8-12 called Art Works every summer. I've been an Artist-in-Residence for the state of Oklahoma since 1980. I go into schools for 2-6 weeks, teach, write plays and create performances with them. Mostly now I travel around the state and direct plays for Community Theatres. I also have been involved with a theatre here called Carpenter Square Theatre for 35 years as a director, performer, and now board president. Right now I'm creating costumes for a 4th grade version of the Jungle Book for Westminster School.

Addendum

Doobie was one of the more permanent apprentices at the Studio, and she always made lasting impressions on everyone. Once when we toured in the old school bus all the way to Georgia, we stopped at my Dad's in North Carolina. Doobie took advantage of the washing machine there and washed everyone's dirty clothes and costumes. Every time after that when I would be in touch with Dad, he'd say, "How's the Little Washer Woman doing?"

On one trip we realized we were going to be too late for dinner at the Studio, so we stopped at a small diner in Darlington, WI to eat. It was the day after the state election. Doobie asked the waitress, "Who won?" The reply was, "Rosie lost."

Suddenly I realized that this was probably the café owned by the wife of Gordon Roseleip, who was notorious for rather stupid public statements. He was known far beyond the state line for making sure that colored margarine would remain illegal in Wisconsin, thus protecting the butter produced from local dairies.

I was afraid that Doobie was going to make some embarrassing remark, so I started kicking her shins under the table. She ignored my warning and responded to the waitress by saying, "Oh that's good isn't it?" My kicks continued to no avail as she then said,

"We wanted him to lose, didn't we?" The waitress looked sadly at Doobie and said, "I suppose a lot of people wanted that."

When the waitress turned and walked away, I said, "Doobie, I'm sure that the waitress is the owner of the restaurant and is Gordon Roseleip's wife."

It had been reported that she had wanted Rosie to win to keep him in Madison and away from her customers in Darlington.

erg

John Aden, Traveling Man

Doobie Potter, Nailed

At the Studio from 1974-1977

Susan Chreitzberg

Susan was at the Valley Studio from 1974 through 1977. During her stay she was a member of the Wisconsin Mime Company, and later on taught at the University of Memphis for over 30 years.

One summer, with all of the students at the Studio, as well as some of the teachers, we decided to do a baseball game. We challenged people from Spring Green to a baseball game. We went into Spring Green where they had a baseball diamond. We came in white face, and some dressed as clowns. We had jugglers. One woman at one point rode a unicycle all around the base paths. (I just thought of this. That same woman could eat a lightbulb. I don't know how she did that!)

Anyway, when one of the opposing players would run the bases, we'd stop them by building a mime wall in front of them. We'd throw mime baseballs around. Now I don't know about the folks from Spring Green, but we had a great time. It must have been 1974 or 1975.

Now during the year, especially during the winter, all of the students would help fix up the Studio. We'd do whatever needed to be done. Reid decided that we needed to paint the whole Studio. We were all painting away, when one woman decided we shouldn't be doing this unless we got paid. She convinced us all to go on strike in order to get paid for painting. We did go on strike for a day, and I think Reid was very upset because all of the students went on strike! He managed to talk us back in to helping again, and the woman decided to leave. I don't know if Reid will remember that or not, the day the students went on strike.

The Valley Studio was a special place. The Studio really changed my way of seeing. It was a powerful mirror that reflected myself back to me in a lot of ways.

BIO

Susan Chreitzberg, now retired, was a professor of physical theatre at the University of Memphis for 32 years. She has taught, performed, choreographed, directed and studied internationally in dance, mime, mask performance, stage combat, acting and Asian Theatre. Earlier in her career she performed professionally with the Mudhead Mime and Mask Theatre, the Wisconsin Mime Theatre, Thomas Leabhart's Corporeal Mime Theatre and the Pendulum Mime Theatre.

Addendum

I don't remember the strike, but I do remember that a student one summer, objected to the assigned chores. She said, "I didn't pay to come here and have to work. I suppose you're assigning these chores to keep the expenses low."

"No that is not the reason, even though it does achieve that. We feel that the chores of kitchen duty, landscaping or garden work are a part of the total learning process . . .bringing together instruction in the arts and everyday self-maintenance."

Her response (she was a school teacher), "I've never heard of such a pedagogy."

It was obvious to me that she would complain for the whole session, if she remained, so I said, "If you're so unhappy with our program, I would be quite happy returning your tuition."

I wasn't happy losing a single red cent, but I knew if she stayed, not only would she be miserable, but she would make everyone else miserable also . . .Miserable people are quite generous, sharing their misery with everyone around them.

She left.

erg

It Changed My Life Totally

Judy Finelli

The Valley Studio was a very dramatic place. It changed my life totally! Hovey Burgess, who was my husband at the time, and I were at the Valley Studio probably in the mid-to-late '70's. We arrived in July, and it was warm. The first thing I noticed was the beauty of the place. The farm was so gorgeous, and the place where we stayed was made of stones and wood: very rustic and different from what we were used to.

I remember that the bell would ring at 6:00 AM. I was used to sleeping later, but I found after a few days that I loved getting up early and having one of those great breakfasts. A lot of that food was from the farm, and it just tasted so good!

Teaching the classes was extraordinary! The students were so spirited and enthusiastic. They were very hungry for the circus work and for any movement work. They were like little sponges. They wanted your life. Of course with such enthusiasm, you gave it to them. You'd teach and they'd stay and work after class. They would even do presentations in the evenings in the main workshop space with the high ceiling.

We hung a trapeze from a tree branch of a big tree down at the bottom of the hill. Students would work on trapeze while hanging from the tree. While you worked on the trapeze, little things from the tree would fall all over you. It was such a joy to do that outdoors. It was so fresh and healthy feeling.

We put up a tight wire between some trees. I still remember watching individual students walking on the tight wire we put up.

That was so great to be able to walk a tight wire outdoors because of the great air and the environment. We had only earlier done it indoors. But here we could do it outdoors! I loved it!

I remember I would go practice on the lawn until it got dark. I would keep juggling as long as I could. I remember how much I loved doing that as the light would get dimmer and dimmer.

And the other teachers! It was so beautiful to watch the late William Burdick teach Period Dance out on the big lawn. Now, it was the second time we had met Leonard Pitt. He was freshly back from Bali, and he was so full of that experience. Watching his class was just lovely and inspirational. So many colorful people. Just wonderful. Little did I know how unique it was.

The longer it gets away from events of that time, the more I think honestly of what it was. It was just intoxicating. I was absolutely drunk with the Valley Studio! Of course we did not appreciate at the time how special it was. What a group of talented people. It was just fabulous!

I love the place. It was a great experience. It was your pleasure to be there.

Post Script:

Through the summers at the Valley studio, I learned to live in nature and with nature in a way. I had never done before. I learned to feel the day - from sunrise to sunset. Feel morning, noon evening and night time in a new way. This has been invaluable in my life. I have had to deal with serious illness and I survived and am still alive in part because I know the rhythms of nature that I first learned at the Valley studio. I did know them as a child, but in growing up - I had forgotten but the Valley studio reminded me.

Hovey and Judy Burgess, Sharing Juggling

A Creative, Supportive Environment

Lesley Powell

I was at the Valley Studio in 1974 and '75. I was nineteen at the time, I think. Reid definitely changed my life. Working with Reid I discovered that I really wanted to be an artist.

The Valley Studio was truly a very creative, supportive environment. It was unlike any other place I'd experienced: very different from my experiences at universities. While there, I had a lovely, fun and creative time. It was very different I think from the summer programs when there were many people at the Studio because we got to perform a lot. While there, I realized that I enjoyed creating new work. I credit Reid for helping me to discover that about myself. At the Valley Studio I also gained the confidence to actually become an artist and performer.

One thing that was really nice was because we were living in the country, we had no distractions. I don't even think we had TV at all. So we were either reading, or rehearsing in the studios, or singing. It was beautiful having no distractions. I remember we had fun making up songs. We'd take current songs, or Beatles' songs, and we'd rewrite the lyrics to be about the three dogs that lived at the Studio. It was fun to be singing.

I remember that Reid would take us through many different types of exercises. Sometimes we'd bring to class characters we'd be working on. We'd then explore these characters outside of our piece, which made them much more three dimensional. This gave a richness to the material that was really special. It lent a better understanding of the character which then affected the piece.

Another thing I remember is that for the year-long program, we had to put on a show at the end of the term. Down the road there was a bunch of rocks that had different spaces between them. I created a performance in that structure. I remember that when I was walking up to my performance it started raining cats and dogs. I came back to the Studio, and after waiting out the rain for an hour or so, we went up there and I did the performance in and around the rocks. I'd do different pieces in different places among the rocks (boulders). A colleague would lead the audience group to where I'd be waiting in one of the spaces, and I'd perform there. The audience would see me perform, then my colleague would lead them to another location and they'd find me in a new place waiting to perform for them once they came there.

I also remember that when we wanted a night out, we'd all go out together. Say we'd go to a bar. Well, we'd all dance together. We had this thing where one person would freeze in a pose and the other person would dance around them and fill in their shape and freeze. We would have eight or nine of us dancing in some Wisconsin bar like this!

Reid was a very profound kind of teacher. Although he was very humble, he knew how to bring strengths out of people: very brilliant in his way with his combination of Asian theater and mime. He knew how to push us as well as support us at the same time while we explored movement, character and gesture in many different ways. That is something I still use today that I learned there: how to challenge people without tearing them down.

I remember that my time at the Valley Studio was a really creative time for me. I am always thankful for the way Reid changed my life and how I approach my work as an artist.

Mamako Yoneyama, Zen Mime Demonstration

It's Difficult, Knowing Where To Begin.

Craig Jacobsen

My first visit to The Valley Studio was in October of 1975. I stopped taking classes following my freshman year (Spring of 1975) at the University of Minnesota – Minneapolis. I was frustrated with taking the required Liberal Arts classes and drowning in the high-density student population (around 70,000, alone at the Minneapolis campus). I wanted something less academic and more focused on the actor. Instead, I took several backstage & front-of-house jobs at the Guthrie Theatre, where I could see all the performances for free. I recalled a dorm mate at the U of MN, from Milwaukee, mentioning a Mime Company based in Wisconsin, which had done a one-week workshop at his high school. I was growing tired of not receiving actor training and wrote The Valley Studio to apply for an apprenticeship to The Wisconsin Mime Company.

In October of 1975, a friend and I hitchhiked down to Spring Green and spent the weekend at a magical and entrancing farm-studio-theater. Most importantly, I met Dr. E. Reid Gilbert, as well as the founding members of The Wisconsin Mime Theatre, John Aden, Susan Chitzberg, Kaye "Doobie" Potter, Marty Schwartz, among others. We participated in workshops centered on Mime, Ballet, Circus Techniques and other movement based arts. On the final day, I presented a short solo piece developed over the weekend, which served as my final audition. In January of 1976, I received my letter of acceptance and prepared to report for classes around the beginning of April. When I arrived to begin my apprenticeship, my life's route was forever changed.

THE PEOPLE

There were so many fine souls at The Valley Studio, some, always present, others, fleeting, but everyone, necessary and grand in nature.

The ever-loving **Nina Edming**, Business Manager and major-domo, her husband Roger and their son & daughter. They lived right down the road on Upper Wyoming Road, in an old farmhouse with a fresh water pond, from which watercress was provided for our Studio meals.

Later on came **Derry Graves**, bringing a smile and a hard-edged dedication to seeing the operations of the Studio and its members flourish. She and her husband, Robert, remained pivotal in my life, for years to come.

Our cook was **Ellen DuPuy** (nee Rubinoff). She was endlessly creative in preparing healthy and creative meals. She also showed profound patience in overseeing many apprentices who were talented in cooking or otherwise as kitchen assistants. Her keen sense of humor and "salt & pepper" approach to commandeering the kitchen and dining room made it a center of social gatherings at all times of the day and night.

In the summer of 1976, as a kitchen assistant, I was in charge of the July 4th lunch. Attempting a stab at patriotism, I recall making apple pies. I created crusts that were red, white & blue. Trying my best to keep it "healthy" the crusts were made from whole-wheat flour. As I recall, they were an epic failure, but nonetheless, as with any food cooked, most of it was eaten. I especially recall the morning hand-made granola w/ yogurt, or kefir breakfasts.

John Aden led a morning yoga class in the main studio each morning, around 6:30, or 7 a.m. The studio, designed by local architect & Frank Lloyd Wright apprentice, Herbert Fritz, had a vaulted ceiling, approximately twenty feet tall, at the highest point, with a membrane of glass windows. It was an inspiring room. On some days, while going through our poses, John's cat, Grendel, would come bounding through the dewy grass, up to the window, with a freshly killed rabbit in her mouth. She would sit there, in front of the window, holding the rabbit, while we were inside trying not to break our collective Zen-yoga focus. John was like a big brother to everyone. I always looked up to him, not only for his talent, but also his earnest sincerity and nurturing approach.

Kay "Doobie" Potter was a firecracker. An accomplished movement artist and clown, she was filled with "piss & vinegar". On my first or second day at the Valley Studio, while taking my shower, she snuck into the bathroom and dropped a relatively large bull snake over the shower curtain into my stall. I have always had an extreme fear of snakes, and to have this thing, which I didn't recognize at first, fall from the ceiling and over my head to the floor, was exhilarating and shocking. I jumped out of the shower before the snake did, screaming and running down the hall to my room, naked and dripping water. Kaye profusely apologized once she discovered my fear of snakes, yet I sensed I had passed some sort of hazing and felt indebted to her for taking the effort to arrange the stunt. Her son, Timmy, was also part of the Studio family. Each of us taking turns spending time with him when Kaye had to teach or go on tour.

Susan Chrieitzberg was our Modern Dance and Ballet instructor. She lived in an apartment underneath the original farmhouse and beneath the offices. Susan hailed from Murfreesboro, TN. She was tall and exceptionally elegant. She always reminded me of Joni Mitchell. She had a talent for getting young, muscle-bound boys, trained in high school sports, to don tights & leotards and do our best to stretch and reach toward the sky. I recall how painful and difficult the dance classes were. I had never before spent so much time stretching my hamstrings and calf muscles. She instilled in me a love for syncopated movement that continued for decades after. Even to the point of having danced the character role of Herr Drosselmeyer in three productions of *The Nutcracker* years later, and studying under Rebecca Wright, of the Joffrey Ballet & American Ballet Theatre.

APPRENTICES AND SUMMER STUDENTS

The "community" of The Valley Studio, subsisted in greatest numbers of those who came to study for either weeks or years. It was a wild confluence of young performance artists from around the world, colliding together in that verdant and peaceful valley.

My first roommate was **Tommy Ukinski**, from Chicago. He was a heart-warming man who reminded me of a young Tom Waits. I was always impressed with his knowledge of philosophy, mixed with a nod of the "school of hard knocks." He had previously studied theology and stand-up comedy before coming to The Valley Studio. I have always felt nothing but warmth and admiration for him. Last I heard, he'd passed his bar exams in Texas and was entering the career of a lawyer.

Kirk Olgin was around during my first year, or so. He was a true "prankster". I recall him hitching into Madison on highway 14 with his cello for lessons. He could make a chair laugh if he wanted to. At the top of the stairs leading from the studio to the dormitory hallway Kirk had epoxied a quarter onto the pine floor, just to look out his room and see everyone passing by stop and look around to see if anyone was looking, then bend over and try to pick it up. To this day I wonder if that quarter is still epoxied to the floor at the top of the steps. He and Tommy Ukinski frequently palled around together.

Joey Daly was a close friend during my Studio years. He was endlessly creative and resourceful. He always kept, among other things, a safety pin on him. He'd say, "You can fix anything with one of these." Once, when we were driving in one of his old trucks, the clutch shift literally disengaged from the floor of the truck. Joe fixed it with a safety pin!

One summer (77?) we spent the summer living in an old farmhouse we were rehabbing over the ridge behind the Studio. It wasn't Lola Richardson's house (that comes later). Well, we had no plumbing or electricity at the old house and each morning we'd wake up and walk the ¾ mile path, over the ridge, to the Studio dining room for breakfast. One morning, walking to the Studio, Joe saw a bull snake inside a rotting log. I feared snakes to death, but Joe couldn't resist going after it. Once he'd extracted the snake, about 4 feet long, from the log, he decided to let it wrap itself around his shirtless waist. He kept it on his torso as we entered the dining room for breakfast, until someone noticed it and screamed. Joe then removed it and let it go outside.

I believe it was in the summer of 78 that he and Janice Wykoff moved into Lola Richardson's house over the ridge. Lola and her brother had been born in the house sometime in the very late 1800's. They remained there until the brother died and Lola went into the nursing home in Dodgeville. The house had never been wired for electricity and had the only propane fueled refrigerator I've ever seen in my life. The driveway, off Hillside School Road was treacherous and over a half mile long, crossing a creek with no bridge. Lola and her brother kept it rough to dissuade visitors. Visiting and staying with them, at the house was like stepping back in time. They had chickens, Janice was weaving then, there was a hand pump in the kitchen for water, and oil lamps for light. I recall the hot and humid summer nights in that house: silent as it was dark. It had a magic all it's own. Later, the house was purchased by Dean Connors and fully updated. Last time I was there, around 2002, it was hardly recognizable but fully occupied, and home to a new nursery company.

One summer, Joe bought a Mayflower moving van and made it his "home-on wheels". He drove it to Austin, TX, and lived in it while there. The Mayflower van was a vehicle of legend and had its final day, I believe, in St. Louis. As I recall, Joe was returning to Wisconsin from somewhere, and the van started to smoke. Joe was downtown and decided to stop and pull over. Once he got out, the van burst into flames. Joe, not wanting to deal with the drama, snuck away as the fire department arrived to douse the flames. He lost all of his tools in the fire. They had all melted due to the extreme heat.

He also borrowed a British car from Bill & Ellen DuPuy (an Austin?). The car ran, but had some shortcomings: like no operating turn lights. For a quick fix Joe rigged two toggle switches, bolted to a chunk of wood and affixed to the dash. When it was time to signal a turn, you would flick the appropriate switch back and forth to make the exterior turn lights work.

Drora Schub & Janice Wykoff were my closest Studio mates. Drora hailed from Chicago, and Janice, from Appleton, WI. We were thick-as-thieves for many years, off and on, during our shared and independent life adventures. I can't find the words to describe the beauty these two souls have. I can say, though, that knowing them has forever forged the path of my life, and I believe continues to do so to this day. We shared several houses and apartments over the years, not only in Spring Green, but in Grand Rapids, MI, too. One couldn't ask for better friends.

E. Reid Gilbert of course, is the person who made all of this possible. He is a very gifted performer, mentor, magnet, ambassador, and all-around magnificent ringleader. Had it not been for Reid, my life would have turned out very different than it has. He opened my eyes to so many things, not only in the disciplines of theater, mime and movement art, but in nature, and more importantly life itself. Reid's compassion allowed me opportunities and provided forgiveness I doubt I could receive anywhere else.

I specifically recall the day I used the Studio station wagon to transport some kittens from the Studio to the farmhouse we were rehabbing. En route, going up County Road ZZ, the kitties scampered to the back of the wagon, and I thought they were going to leap out of the hatchback window, which didn't work and was wide open. Reaching back and trying to grab their tails and keep them from leaping out, I drove the station wagon right off a bridge and over a shallow creek: landing in a farmer's swamp and field. The car was totaled and the kitties were nowhere to be found. I didn't realize what at first had taken place. Then I looked up and saw that the gravel rose four feet above me and there was a gaping break in the bridge railing where I'd driven the car through. I walked back to the Studio and sheepishly went into the office to tell Nina I had wrecked the Studio car. I was certain that I would be banished from the Studio and told to pack my bags. Nina said that Reid wouldn't be back until after dinner and that I should clean up and rest. I could see him in the evening. Reid returned around 9 pm that night and I sulked down to his apartment, sure that my days at the Studio were over. My stomach was in knots. I knocked on the door. Reid invited me in warmly and asked what was on my mind. I sputtered out what I'd done and waited for his reply. He sat silently in his chair for several moments and then said, "Well, you better try to find the cats in the morning and make sure to get a good night's rest. Was there anything else you need to discuss?" I said, "No," and, "I'm sorry," and walked out into the summer night convinced I was the most fortunate person on the planet. The next day I found the kitties and returned to classes. Reid never mentioned the event again, aside from saying a year later, that from totaling the wagon he'd received $4,000 in insurance, which was far more than the car was worth to begin with. Ha!

To close this out, I first want to list the names of those I remember, apprentices and instructors, as they were a part of the fabric of it all (forgive the name misspellings, but it's been nearly 40 years):

John Towsen, Karen Flaherty, Tom and Sally Leabhart, Steven Wasson, Hovey Burgess, Avner The Eccentric, James Roose Evans, James & Marty van Eaman, Smokey (the Labrador), William "Iggy" Freeman, Craig Silvey, JoAnne Sherman, Terry Kerr, Joe Long, Nan Ducklow, Ted Lang, All The Folks From Adelphi University, Bond Street Theater Coalition, Dom Robinson, Bill DuPuy, Phyllis Dyer, Meg Cunningham, Patty Weizchek, Drew Richardson, Bill Rauch, Christine Michaels, Edna Meudt (and she Meudt not), Jo Anderson, Carlo Mazzone Clemente, Laurie Aden . . .

There are countless others, which I'm embarrassed to say, I can't remember at this moment, but each and every person that passed through the portal of the Valley Studio School of Mime left an indelible imprint on my psyche and my soul, for which, I will be forever thankful. The "magic" of the Studio was the coming together of so many creative minds from every corner of the world, colliding in a moment: a confluence of spirits young and old, timeless in its happening and lasting a life time in my heart. I will hold dear every memory I have from those years and know that because of what I did and saw there, that there is always a chance and a great probability it can and will happen again and again because it should.

Thank you one and all, and especially E. Reid Gilbert, for a whole life bottled into the span of three short and power-packed years, they were, to coin a phrase, "Lightning-in-a-bottle."

Addendum

A PS to Craig's story. Smokey and I also lived in the Lola house with Janice and Joey.

One beautiful spring morning when Smokey and I were walking over to the Studio from the Lola house, I was overwhelmed with the scene when we were crossing the old pasture. I looked down the valley to see the fog-enshrouded Wisconsin River, and right in front of me was an apple tree in full blossom. On a low branch of the tree sat a scarlet tanager preening his coat.

I was unable to go any farther as long as that gorgeous bird was performing there for me. So I figured that if I got closer he would just fly away. I walked slowly toward him, but he only continued his morning ritual. I finally had to go right up to him and tell him to leave, which he thoughtfully did. If he hadn't left I would have been there all morning.

The other house on the corner of Schoolhouse Road and ZZ was occupied by several guys, some not affiliated with the Studio. There was a wonderful old barn there, where we stored our portable stage. Unfortunately someone stole that stage one weekend when we were all gone.

I also stored there several pieces of walnut wood, which Edna Meudt had given me. She had hired a fellow to saw and chop up some wood for winter. Much to her dismay, he had sawed down a dry walnut tree and had cut it up in chunks for firewood. When she discovered what he had done, she gave all that wood to me for carving. When I put it into that barn I told the guys that they were not to burn any of that as it was going to be used for art projects. However when spring came, I went to inspect my treasure trove of walnut, only to discover that that had been stolen also

I knew very well that those lazy critters in the house didn't have enough gumption to go cut their own wood. If I knew who was responsible for burning that wonderful walnut wood, I would not have been as forgiving as I was with Craig and the demolished Studio car.

erg

An Unintended, Unexpected Influence on My Life

Judith Cohn Britt

I attended the Valley Studio for two short sessions: one in the summer and one in the winter. It was there that I met John Towsen, among other people.

The Valley Studio had an unintended, unexpected influence on my life. It was in many ways because of meeting David Harper, a Deaf man, that I became a sign language interpreter. David taught me a few signs ("My turtle is dead", being the most notable, although there were some rather unflattering sign names he attempted to give me, reflecting my, *ahem* proportions!).

David and I kept in contact for a while after we left the Valley Studio, and filmed for a kid's TV show in New Orleans, of which I had been a part of during high school. David was good friends with another guy at our workshop, Tim Adair.

Because of my training at the Valley Studio, as well as Celebration Mime Theatre, the transition from physical performance to sign language interpretation was a relatively easy one. I had become disillusioned with the idea of having to audition repeatedly in order to find work, and the hours were killing me...not to mention the prospect of holding two or more jobs so that I didn't starve. When I moved to Seattle, WA, in 1990, I had theatrical friends from Antioch College living there (Shannon Wood and Peter Kurland), who had worked with the National Theatre for the Deaf. It was they who suggested that perhaps I would be interested in taking some sign language classes at the community college. With the foundation of my studies in physical performance, David Harper's influence and introduction into the Deaf world, and the suggestion of my friends, I enrolled in night classes to learn ASL. Thirty years later, I am still a sign language interpreter, specializing in performance interpreting.

Another memory from the Valley Studio was when Ken Feit taught storytelling. It must have been a clear night and a full moon, because the moonlight streamed through the huge glass windows of the Frank Lloyd Wright inspired architecture. We all lay on the wooden floor, with the large wooden rafters dimly lit from the moonlight, as he played a recording of Gordon Bok's "Peter Kagan and the Wind". The story completely transported me; I cannot tell you the magic of that evening. To this day, I cannot listen to that Selkie Story without crying.

Another note about Ken: I wish I had kept all of the beautiful paper animals that Ken created. He gave me a virtual menagerie of critters that he cut and folded in the blink of an eye. Ken was a remarkable man. When I heard that he had died in a car accident, I called John Towsen immediately. Unfortunately, I was living in a time zone three hours earlier than he, and woke him up at some ungodly hour. Naturally, he already knew.

My Valley Studio Story

Louisa Gluck

In 1976 during my second semester at Beloit College in Beloit, Wisconsin, a mime troupe came to perform. John Aden and Doobie Potter were amongst those on stage. As they described the Valley Studio Mime School and the organic garden and classes, I felt inspired to enroll for the summer. I had never lived in community before. The experience at Valley Studio shaped my life in many ways beyond the world of mime.

I stayed for Summer and Fall 1976 and Spring 1977. Some of my teachers were:

Reid Gilbert, Thomas and Sally Leabhart, William Burdick, Carlo Alessandro Luigi Mazzone-Clementi, Nilima Devi, James Roose-Evans, Hovey Burgess, Leonard Pitt, Mamako Yoneyama, and Ken Feit. I loved having teachers from around the world with different theatrical styles. Classes included: Acting, Corporeal Mime, Ballet, Jazz dance, Renaissance dance, Commedia dell'arte, Kathak Classical Indian dance, Mask making, Circus technique, Experimental theatre, Mime and Zen, Storytelling and Composition.

I lived in a tent, or sometimes in a teepee on the hill, and when it was cold, in the dorms. During time off, I biked to the Wisconsin River to swim. Not far from VS was a beautiful spiritual community called Willow Gold. I attended some of their healing events and remained in touch with the founder, Marion Nelson, for several years. This experience also strongly impacted my life. Willow Gold became Medicine Buddha Healing Center, Mahayana Dharma Center and later, Global View.

Recently I re-read the journals I wrote at VS and beyond. In retrospect I can see I was in overwhelm mode a lot of the time. I had conversations with so many people and was constantly learning new things everyday. I was learning about caring for the body and the mind as a performer. I was feeling the challenge of making career and lifestyle decisions. I had many diverse interests and was struggling with shaping myself as an adult. I was being influenced on many levels: theatre, politics, sexuality, nutrition, spirituality and world travel.

Living in a small community and studying together in small classrooms was extremely intimate. Being a private person and more of an introvert than an extrovert created a dynamic tension for me. To compensate for living in a fishbowl, I cut a lot of classes to find solitary time to reflect, read, rejuvenate and have time away from community life. My mind was not set on being a dancer, a mime, an actress or a clown. I was exploring the idea of using movement in theatre. I was aware of being self-conscious and the challenge of establishing confidence in myself as a performer. Most present in my being was a deep need to explore on a spiritual level. My father had died when I was 17 years old and within a few months I had left my parents' home.

I had not anticipated meeting a mystical teacher at VS. However one of the teachers had a very profound impact on my life. When Ken Feit performed at Beloit College in June 1976, I was already at the Valley Studio. For those who don't know Ken, he had studied to be a Jesuit Priest. At age 26 he left the Priesthood to be with a woman and then the woman left him. Ken visited his friend, Daniel Berrigan, the famous counter-culture peace activist, who was in prison. Daniel encouraged him to go to clown school. Taking his advice, Ken studied at Barnum and Bailey Clown College and eventually became known as a Priestly Fool.

At the VS Ken was teaching Elizabeth Kubler Ross' five stages of grief. This was like finding an oasis in the desert. He performed mystical vignettes using a tiny suitcase filled with balloons, bananas and other implements of impermanence. He created haikus using sign language and/or exaggerated sounds. I remember one lovely haiku about the rising moon that he had used to save himself from potential muggers. As he mimed the haiku he used a screechy, crazy voice that drove the muggers away, thinking he was insane. Ken was exploring the human condition and emotions in a unique way in a culture that was only slowly beginning to face the inner world.

Ken wore a denim jacket with all sorts of things attached to it: pacifiers, buttons, badges, etc.

He was 36 years old and I was 19. We became friends and visited together over the years. Ken invited me to travel with him to India, however the timing was not right. You can read his travel letters on John Towsen's blog: http://physicalcomedy.blogspot.com/2012/10/the-travel-letters-of-ken-feit.html

After Ken's travels he visited me at college and brought water from the Ganges River. I still have his letters along with his origami unicorns and elephants.

On April Fool's Day in 1981 Ken wrote a letter inviting me to travel the world with him for a mixture of research, pilgrimage, performance and adventure. We were at a crossroads in our relationship. He wrote that if I wasn't willing to commit on a deeper level, he wanted to end our friendship. Therefore, due to our different desires at the time, our relationship ended with this letter.

A few months later, I got a call from Janet Evans, a friend from VS, who had been driving with Ken from California to Wisconsin. On the day after my 24th birthday, in the early morning, Ken had fallen asleep at the wheel. Janet was sleeping in the back seat surrounded by sleeping bags, duffel bags and her art supplies. She told me she had woken up to the sound of water. The car had driven off the road and landed in a stream. The bamboo pole that Ken had used for death rituals had punctured him in the ribs. Janet got out and flagged down a truck. In the ambulance, on the way to the hospital, Ken said to Janet – "Please stop talking, I'm dying." How shocking it was to have just said goodbye and to hear that Ken was truly gone.

Later I heard he had proposed to a Canadian woman at the

same time he had written to me and she had said yes. Janet created a beautiful drawing of a knotted piece of wood flying out of a doorway.

An excerpt from a letter Janet wrote me:

> *I clearly remember the year that he sent out his 40th birthday letter, which included his preparations for his "death journey." (In fact, I think I still have the letter) He had been doing so much international traveling at that time, much of it in dangerous parts of the world, that I interpreted his letter as just another layer in his study of the life/death process. Sure, it had a slightly eerie tinge to it, as any reflection of one's own death would; but I wasn't sure that it was an omen of things to come (as some other people had opined). I don't remember ever hearing him foresee his own death by car accident, but I do remember hearing Ken say that he would, most likely, die while "on the road." But his whole life was itinerant at that time, so that made sense to me — if he was traveling all the time, of course death would find him traveling.*

A year after Ken's death, I moved to Japan. This is an excerpt from a book I am currently writing. VS and Ken continued to influence my life:

> *I read in the Tokyo Journal that a couple living on a bio-dynamic organic farm were performing mime at a theatre called La Mama. I had studied mime in Wisconsin at The Valley Studio Mime School when I was 19 and had worked in their organic garden, so I was curious and eager to meet these performers. While walking toward the venue with a Japanese friend, uncertain where we were going, we heard a man's voice, in English, say - Are you lost? A very handsome Japanese couple approached. They were also going to La Mama. It turned out this man's sister owned the farm and the mime performers were her friends. He had been watching them rehearse for months and hadn't planned to attend the performance, but the woman he was with persuaded him. They were lead actors in a play. When he first approached I felt I had known him for a million years. He seemed so familiar. After*

the performance, he gave me his phone number, in crayon. I was smitten. This encounter resulted in a relationship that took the two of us on many adventures in Japan, Thailand, Burma, Nepal, Sri Lanka, Singapore and in the USA and Canada.

Two people who I have remained in contact with from VS are Tanja Anselm-Cooke and Janet Evans. Janet and I did a clown gig after VS and I recently found the receipt for the payment. $15! Tanja and I reconnected many years later. She had remained in contact with Joe Daly. In 2012, the three of us got together. Tanja and I located Jonathan Haglund and reconnected with him on the phone. I hope you will be able to read all of their stories here.

Another teacher from VS whom I met again was Leonard Pitt. I heard him on the radio while I was living in the San Francisco Bay area and went to visit him at his unique home. More recently I've been enjoying his posts on Facebook of historic Paris and his studies with Decroux.

Living in Spring Green and studying at the Valley Studio was an incredible, magical time that I will always remember and cherish. Re-reading my journals I have even more appreciation and gratitude for Reid's perseverance and dedication in creating an artistic community and inviting so many remarkable, inspirational teachers from around the world.

BIO:

The time I spent at VS transferred to Beloit College as theatre credits. During the winter break, I studied in NYC – modern dance at Martha Graham's studio, jazz dance with Pepsi Bethel, ballet with Zena Rommett and creative dance with Maggie Beals. I later studied dance choreography at the University of Wisconsin at Madison. And I spent the summer studying poetry and writing at Goddard College in Vermont. Upon graduating from Beloit, I travelled in Europe and the Middle East. I lived with the Moonies while attending The Edinburgh Theatre Festival, which reminded me of VS days. I spent a day at Findhorn Community in Scotland. I visited a friend who was studying opera in Germany. I picked apples and avocados on a kibbutz in Israel, saw the pyramids in Egypt, etc.

I was fortunate to be in Wisconsin in 1981 when His Holiness the Dalai Lama gave his first Kalachakra Initiation in the USA. This led to further studies in Tibetan Buddhism and attending many of His Holiness' teachings in the USA and India.

In the early 80's I lived in Japan, taught English, travelled in Asia and began sponsoring two Tibetan children I met in Nepal. From Japan I returned to the USA and travelled in Canada with my Japanese boyfriend. We lived for a short while in British Columbia with Karen Schnabel, another friend from VS. Eventually I landed in upstate NY and lived in a Zen Monastery for three years. From there I made my way to California and studied in a spiritually based graduate school. I received a Masters degree in Counseling Psychology and spent many years gathering hours to obtain the California Marriage and Family Therapist license. Upon completion, I returned to Thailand, India, and Nepal spending time with the Tibetan children I had sponsored, who were now adults. I went on Pilgrimage to various Buddhist sites and received teachings from several Buddhist masters.

While I was living in Japan I discovered Aikido, a non-violent Martial Art. Back in the USA, I was able to train for several years at a beautiful dojo in Northern California. A memorable job I had was as tour manager for the Maitreya Project Relic Tour. I traveled across America and Canada for 6 months presenting the relics at different venues. If you would like to see if the relics will be in your area, here is the website: http://www.maitreyarelictour.com. Currently I am writing a book that weaves together tales of how Buddhism has impacted my life.

Ken Feit, A Fool for the Lord

Craig Silvey, Simply Smiley

Nearly 40 Years Since My Valley Studio Experience

Janet Evans

I'm thrilled that a compilation of stories from the Valley Studio is being organized. Thank you to Reid Gilbert, Jef Lambdin and all who are working to make it happen! Although I only attended the Valley Studio for the summer of 1976, the experiences and insights I gained from that short time have deeply enriched my life and continues to inform my work today – nearly 40 years later.

I was introduced to the Valley Studio thanks to Ken Feit and the generosity of a woman named Connie Banks. As a sophomore studying visual art and art education at UW-Madison I attended a retreat led by Ken Feit on campus, November 7 – 8, 1975. It included an evening performance followed by a full-day workshop the next day. In his performance Ken used the simplest of props to conjure whole new worlds of perception, and his workshop revealed a creative process that stemmed from a profound and honest exploration of the human condition. In short, Ken's creative approach offered what I had been seeking in my art studies: the philosophical tools to critically discern the world around and within me, and the freedom to explore and develop the best way to express my perceptions. I was hooked.

Though I had no theater experience at all, I knew I had stumbled onto something deep and valuable that I had to pursue. An acquaintance, Connie, had registered for another workshop that was to occur a few weeks later at the Valley Studio on the weekend of Nov

21-23. When she had to withdraw from that workshop she asked the Valley Studio to apply her down-payment toward my registration. Since I was paying for my college education, and therefore extremely broke, I was grateful to Connie for helping to make it possible for me to attend. If I remember correctly, the weekend included a performance by Clown Dimitri at Viterbo College in LaCrosse, WI. The poetic beauty of Dimitri's performance truly moved me and furthered my desire to explore physical theater as a form of expression. The whole experience inspired me to attend the Valley Studio that summer of 1976.

I remember driving from Madison through the lush and gently rolling landscape, along progressively smaller and quieter country roads. Not far from Frank Lloyd Wright's Taliesin I turned onto the dirt road that eventually delivered me to the Valley Studio. As I arrived I was delighted to see the large garden, the outdoor stage, the charming barn studio to the right, and the lovely Studio complex with the office, dorms, and kitchen to the left.

The dorms were all filled at the Valley Studio that summer of 1976 so several of us camped. With my tent pitched on a hill on the other side of the woods my daily commute to the Studio was an adventure – especially at night! Smokey, the Studio dog, often joined me on these treks through the wilderness, which I appreciated. About midway along the wooded path was a unique tree that had an interesting story about it – something ghoulish about two sisters, if I remember correctly. Whether an ancient Indian legend (as I was told), or one of Reid's wonderfully inventive tales (which I suspected), the story of that distinct tree added to the magic of that time.

Living in a tent allowed me to fully appreciate the inspiring beauty of the landscape. Waking at dawn to the fresh scent of morning dew, I looked forward to the daily 6am yoga class before breakfast and a full day of classes. Some days were so hot that our toes splashed in little pools of our own sweat as we did our rond de jambs! After our communal dinner the languid evenings were filled with stories, jokes and music. I still laugh when I remember

Joe Goldfield's Bronx rendition of Hamlet "To be or ain't. Now I ask ya.... Me ol' man got knocked off de odda day... His own brodda poured mecuricome in 'is ear..."

Apparently, the Studio had an agreement with neighboring farmers because one morning I awoke to a herd of cows grazing around my tent! After our mutual surprise the cows returned to their nonchalant ennui and I trotted off to my full day of classes. That evening I returned to find that my tent had been trampled. It seems that even bored cows occasionally get rowdy!

The Studio seemed to have good relations with several of the neighbors in the area. There were the occasional visits by people from Taliesin (a woman with her little dog) and I remember attending a party at a nearby farm with lots of dancing in the barn – specifically, clogging.

An impressive international cast of instructors offered a wide array of truly excellent classes at the Valley Studio that summer. Regardless of my exceptionally limited knowledge and experience in theater, mime and dance, I dove into the diverse offerings as if they were my last meal on earth:

Nillima Devi: Kathak Classical Dance of India. Nillima was a true inspiration. She expanded my understanding and appreciation of Indian culture and Hindu philosophy as she helped us relate to the stories that we danced.

Mamako Yoneyama: Japanese Zen Mime. Mamako taught me how to make the invisible visible – how to physically express the spiritual and psychological.

Leonard Pitt: Indonesian Mask Mime. Leonard introduced me to the idea of working the whole body as one unified muscle to communicate a state of mind or a type of character. I was inspired to explore the Indonesian masks and other Indonesian art forms, such as their puppetry and Gamelan music.

Carlo Mazzone Clementi: Commedia dell'arte. I learned to respect the long history and continued relevance of the Commedia characters as I began to recognize aspects of them in myself and others.

James Roose-Evans: Experimental Theater. James honed my understanding of the creative process by identifying a central concept and expanding on it through creative investigation to arrive at a wholly unique way to communicate the concept. I was deeply impressed with the depth and breadth of his knowledge and inventiveness.

William Burdick: Period movement. I learned about the history of Western dance and the physical and psychological discipline that is the foundation of clean movement. Prior to that class I had never considered how difficult it is to simply walk with conscientious intent!

Hovey Burgess: Circus Techniques. Once I learned to juggle I became addicted to any and all circus techniques! I tried everything Hovey offered: tight wire, slack wire, rola bola, rolling globe, diabolo, devil stick, plate spinning, unicycle, and all sorts of juggling.

Sally Leabhart: Ballet and Pilates. I will never forget what I learned from Sally about the anatomy and correct manipulation of the spine. This knowledge helped me recover from traumatic spine injuries in August 1977 and 1981 (see below).

Thomas Leabhart: Corporeal Mime. Learning the physical syntax of the mind/spirit – how the psyche expresses itself in the body.

There were also classes in stage combat that were fascinating to watch, though I didn't participate.

The fellow students and core troupe members were also very inspiring. I remember watching them with awe and admiration for their dedication, spunk and drive.

After that magical summer I returned to my studies in art and art education at UW-Madison but I also continued juggling, dancing, doing yoga, and clowning. I spent the spring semester of 1977 studying with Ken Feit at the state college in Ann Arbor, Michigan. A fellow classmate there named Pamela Hoffman told me about Celebration Mime Theater, so the summer of 1977 found me in South Paris, Maine learning with Tony Montanaro and the brilliant instructors and students there.

In August of 1977, shortly after leaving the Celebration Mime Theater, I fell off a galloping horse and sustained severe nerve and tissue damage in my lower spine. My doctors said the excessive scar tissue in my lumbar would give me trouble for the rest of my life. Thankfully, my prior activities in dance, mime and circus skills gave me the knowledge and conditioning to guide me through many grueling months of recovery. Eventually, I regained the ability to dance and over the years I have taken care and remained active so that I continue to enjoy flexibility and strength.

The spring and summer of 1978 were filled with travel to Europe and the Middle East. Of direct relation to the Valley Studio were my visits to Switzerland and Holland. While in Switzerland my visit to Dimitri's charming studio was a lovely and memorable experience (Scuola Teatro Dimitri, in Verscio, near Locarno). In Amsterdam I visited Lenie, Rene and Sjoerd, three Dutch performers who had attended the Valley Studio at the same time I did in 1976. Sjoerd was involved with a theater company that was performing at the time so I had the good fortune to see him perform. Indonesian arts and cuisine are prevalent in Amsterdam because of their shared history with the Dutch so, with Leonard Pitt in mind, I bought an Indonesian wayan kulit (shadow puppet) and a wayang golek (wooden rod puppet) that inspired me for many years. Attending the "Festival of Fools" in Amsterdam introduced me to a whole new world of international talent. Travels to Jordan, Israel and Syria introduced me to artists and poets of all ages, genders and creeds who were living evidence of the generative and healing power of the arts.

After acquiring my undergraduate degree in 1979 I taught art in the Poynette public school district for five years (20 miles NE of Madison, WI) and continued to dance, juggle and do yoga. I kept in touch with Ken Feit as he travelled around the world and also with others I had met at the Valley Studio: Louisa Gluck, Joe Martinez, and Peter Schreiner, to name a few. At one point I was hired to do clowning for a festival in Madison and I asked Louisa to join me. We had a blast that day and got paid for it! Louisa went on to live in Japan for several years and did a lot of international travel before settling in the San Francisco Bay Area. Joe continued in martial arts and stage combat and taught at colleges. Peter moved to LA to pursue his acting career. In addition to a number of stage performances, he played a recurring character named "Pete" on the popular TV show *Cheers*. I've long since lost touch with Joe and Pete and others from the Valley Studio so I am grateful that Louisa and I have continued to stay in touch. Louisa is the one who told me about this book project. Thank you, Louisa!

The summer of 1981 ended in a horrible car accident that killed Ken Feit and injured me for months. I had decided to spend the summer in San Francisco and Ken had several performances and workshops in the Bay area that summer, so we agreed to drive there together in June and return to the Midwest together in August. In the early morning of August 8, in the Wasatch Mountains about 13 miles east of Heber City, Utah our car ran off the narrow mountain road, down a steep embankment, and landed in a small stream. I had been asleep in the back seat protected by soft sleeping bags and duffle bags, which saved my life. Ken was badly injured but breathing and able to speak. The car doors were jammed shut by boulders and trees but I managed to slip through a small area where the windshield had popped out and scramble up the embankment to flag down any passersby. It took over an hour for the ambulance to reach us and for the EMTs to extract Ken from the car. He passed shortly after arriving at the hospital. Within six months I had basically recovered from the cervical myofascial spinal injury I sustained from the accident, but it took me many years to get over Ken's death and the fact that I had survived. I felt both cursed and blessed to have been the one with him at his time of passing. Ken was only 41 years old and was planning to get married that year. Considering the breadth of his travels and his positive impact on so many people around the world, one might imagine the weight of responsibility that I felt. My art helped me to process the experience and one of my drawings from that time still hangs on my wall to remind me to make good use of my life.

In 1984 I moved to New York City where I made my living as a visual artist for sixteen years until moving to Miami, FL in 2000. While in NYC the lessons I had learned at the Valley Studio continued to inform my visual arts and I continued to orbit the worlds of dance and theater. I worked for a while in the film industry and did a bit of freelance costume, prop and puppetry work. I was surprised one day to encounter Tarn Magnuson in the NYC subway! Although Tarn and I had not attended the Valley Studio at the same time, we had attended the same elementary and middle-school.

In Florida I acquired a Masters degree and taught at the University of Miami for a few years. Currently I am a program director with Arts for Learning, a nonprofit that uses the arts to inspire and teach. We partner with actors, dancers, musicians, visual artists and storytellers to serve early childhood centers, K-12 schools, parks, museums, aspiring teen artists, and people with special needs. As I oversee the design and implementation of a variety of programs I am privileged to witness the positive power of the arts in the lives of those we serve. It's my tenth year with Arts for Learning and I hope to enjoy another ten years! Come visit us if you are ever in Miami!

Reflecting on the trajectory of my life over the past 40 years I realize how meeting Ken Feit and attending the Valley Studio launched me onto a path full of meaning and discovery. Thank you, Reid Gilbert, for having had the vision and the perseverance to make the Valley Studio such a vibrant reality! Forty years ago I had no idea what it took to establish and run a Studio and keep it alive, but I was sure glad that it existed. Now, with a deeper understanding of what you had accomplished, I am all the more grateful to you and to all who contributed to that vision and who continue to celebrate what we shared together through the Valley Studio days.

Ken and Janet, new friends

Valley Studio mud bath

Ken Feit, a Fool for the Lord

E. Reid Gilbert

Ken Feit, a frequent visitor to Valley Studio, was a tall, handsome Jesuit seminarian, studying to enter the Roman Catholic priesthood. The staff and students always looked forward to his visits, as he was such a wonderful storyteller, sharing with us his adventures of hitchhiking across continents in search of storytellers, clowns and fools. He sometimes found them in trees with bright metal objects hanging from the branches. He had traveled across Africa, South America and Australia on his quest.

After Ken finished seminary, he petitioned the bishop of Milwaukee to appoint him as the "Official Fool to the Church." When Ken related this to me he was obviously deeply troubled over the bishop's refusal. I attempted to reassure him of the efficacy of his calling; "Well, Ken, you know the unofficial fools are always more effective in the Church than the official fools." He seemed to take some comfort in that.

Ken was wearing his much-patched denim jacket when he was entertaining some New York ghetto children. One of the kids commented on his jacket, "Man, that coat is ba-ad."

Ken was somewhat abashed at this remark and said, "Why are you saying that? I like this jacket. These patches are souvenirs from all over the world."

"Man, that's what I'm a sayin'. It's really ba-ad." That was when Ken realized that "bad" means "good" when it's spoken in two syllables; "ba-ad." He celebrated new languages generated by the younger generation.

Ken's parents visited the school once while Ken was also there. When Ken wasn't within earshot, Mrs. Feit asked me, "If you didn't know Ken has gone to seminary, would you know that he had gone to seminary?"

At first this inverted tautology stunned me, but I answered, "Well, Mrs. Feit, a person may not know specifically that Ken had gone to seminary, but anyone who knows him at all, will realize that he is a very spiritual person." This seemed to reassure her of the value of his investment in religious studies.

On his storytelling occasions Ken would often take from his duffel bag a paper sack, from which he would extricate a spoon into which he would pour a couple of drops of oil. He would then put in a kind of seed before lighting a candle, which he held under the spoon. While he talked of transformations of life, we waited anxiously for the expected explosion of one grain of popcorn. Pop! Celebration! Transformation! Something quite different had hopped out of the spoon and into the air. Unfortunately, no clown was sitting close enough to catch it in his mouth.

Ken's wish was, "I want to unhinge the mind from the definition of things it has been civilized into."

"But Ken", we might respond, "we continue to strive desperately for such definitions in order to communicate in a rational manner."

"All I'm trying to do is find universal symbols that kind of tickle people to the threshold of a personal query and just leave it there. I direct my actions toward those who are afraid of themselves, locked into routines, trapped, despairing."

One late summer afternoon at Valley Studio, Ken confided to me that he had a problem. Raising myself to an increased counseling stature in Ken's shadow, I asked if I might help. He said that he didn't know what to do with his two original hand puppets, whom he had retired. Their button eyes had already been transplanted to younger puppets, but he couldn't bring himself to throw them away in the garbage. However, his traveling luggage had to be as light as possible.

I suggested a cremation. A crowd soon gathered. Ken and his

eyeless puppets led a procession under a canopy of white fabric – retrieved from the costume shop – down past the garden to the creek. The fabric was an eight yard length of nylon. Any onlooker may have seen us as a huge serpent winding its way down the slope to the water.

We built a fire on a sandbar. Ken laid the puppets on the funeral pyre with loving respect. The felt fabric simply shrank and turned charcoal black while retaining their original shapes.

While they were still aflame I found a stick to place them in the water. As the puppets sank slowly into the creek, the water gurgled bubbles and steam rose silently to join the clouds . . .a heavenly ascension.

Our paths crossed several times after that; usually at the Clown, Mime, Puppet Ministry Workshops, where people from all faith persuasions, including Baptists, Jews, Methodists, Catholics, and Muslims, came to celebrate their individual religious faiths through performance venues.

At the workshop, held at Oberlin College, Ken and I accompanied by our mutual friend, Avner Eisenberg, discovered a secluded lake near the campus. We decided to go skinny dipping there in a celebration of ecumenicity – a Methodist minister, a Jesuit priest and a Jewish clown, stripped, literally, of all external baggage or pretensions. Unfortunately our friends, Islamic Jamal Mohammed and Southern Baptist Billy Bob Jones, weren't there to participate in our ecumenical celebration of water immersion.

In August, 1981, I had arrived at American University in Washington for our annual Workshop. Margie Brown sought me out and asked me, "Have you heard about Ken?"

"I haven't talked with Ken for several months," I replied.

She said, "Maybe we ought to sit down . . . Ken was killed last Friday in an automobile accident."

I was not prepared for this news. Apparently he had fallen asleep while driving somewhere in California. His traveling companion, knowing that he was seriously injured, attempted to assist him. His response to her was, "Quiet, please! I'm dying."

Janet Evans

Another friend, Joseph Martin, celebrated Ken's life by publishing a book, *Foolish Wisdom,* containing stories, activities and reflections from Ken Feit.

Even in the hushed whisper of death, Ken seemed to celebrate us back into the wise foolishness of life.

I Look Back on Those Times

Tanja Anselm-Cooke

I was at the Valley Studio for two full winters and several summers, with the last year being 1977. As well as a great place to study mime and other movement arts, it was a great place for self-discovery. For me, while I was there, just being in a place where I could study how the body could speak and move was just heavenly.

I look back at those times and see how they absolutely affected me. Now I am in a traditional role of being a nurse and I realize that many skills I picked up at the Valley Studio, I still use. One example is the exercise when we'd be all be in the studio running like mad without bumping into each other. I cannot even tell you how often I've used that skill in a subway station or the metro lines or being a nurse running to get to a patient while avoiding all of the things in my way. I use that skill all the time.

Also at the Valley Studio, because we were constantly working on communicating with our bodies. I realized how much I could understand a person by watching their body language and their eyes. So when I was in France (*Studying with Etienne Decroux, 1978-80.*) I found that my ability to understand the eyes, the tone of voice, and the body language of people helped me immensely to understand what they were saying to me. To this day this skill helps me as a nurse to understand the needs of patients who speak another language.

My experience at the Valley Studio has even affected me as a parent. While there I learned to really trust my body. I rarely got hurt. I was able to do all kinds of things because I knew my body really well. The environment of the Valley Studio really enhanced that. So as a parent, I did not restrict my daughter from trying things. I saw my job as not to keep her from getting injured, but to keep her from getting hurt. So she was always more of a daredevil than all of the kids her age. She had a body that she could trust. That was something that came out of the time I spent there.

There is a sense about storytelling when you're part of being able to tell a bigger story, it brings a sense of community and connection. While I was at the Valley Studio, I felt that I was a part of a much bigger story, especially at a really fascinating and exciting time in American history. I felt really fortunate. As a student at the Valley Studio I was able to learn to be passionate and authentic and to make mistakes and to fall down and still be safe. It was such an enchanted place to be able to be. And a lot of it had to do with the person who started it all, Reid.

Since Reid was sort of a "Pied Piper of Lost Souls," The Valley Studio was actually a place where you had this eclectic assortment of really talented human beings. I remember that there was one night at dinner when with only an eggplant and two kumquats, a guy told the entire story of Great Expectations! There was another person there who had very long toes, and he decided that it would be interesting to learn to type with his feet, so he worked on it. I remember that so many of the people there were truly Renaissance people. They all had so many talents: from playing guitar to fixing cars to walking on stilts. One of the guys even helped to restore some carousel horses.

My memory of those years is filled with all of these incredibly meaningful people coming and going. Some people would leave and return, and when they'd come back we'd have a shared history. The souls of some of those people are still with me. They are still the love of my life and I remain connected to them: some loosely but others more strongly. They mean so much to me. Because we were working in the theater, we were all working in the same direction. Even today we're still all working toward something.

Lawn gathering

One Summer's Day in a Mayflower Moving Van

Karen Flaherty

I was at Valley Studio from 1976 – 1978. I arrived there one late summer's day in a Mayflower Moving Van that several of us from Fayetteville, Arkansas purchased to move us out of Fayetteville to the next stages of our life. Owning and driving that van was great fun. Eventually Joe Daly purchased it. Last I heard it was a good old dog for several years but mysteriously caught fire with Joe's belongings in it – sorry to say – and the ashes are buried somewhere between Wisconsin and Michigan.

Prior to VS, I had been a student of Decroux Corporeal Mime with Tom Leabhart at the University of Arkansas and part of the Arkansas Mime Theatre. We had received an invitation from Reid Gilbert to merge with the Wisconsin Mime Theatre and to be a part of the Valley Studio School. Really, Tom did the teaching while we did the rehearsing. Well, Tom rehearsed too – Table, Chair and Glass, The Washerwoman, The Carpenter.

My impressions of Reid were that he was a gracious gentleman with big dreams, aspiration and vision. A kind soul with a passion for inclusive theatre – a space where all disciplines and practices were welcome. But in return you had to participate in all communal activities from mess hall to classes to yard work. And then there was Smokey – if he liked you then you were in like Flynn.

Graciousness was a quality that was shared by all members

of the Wisconsin Mime Theatre. We Decroux "disciples" were interlopers after all. The company included Doobie, John Aden, Susan Chrietzberg . Tom, Meg Partridge, James Van Eman, Robert Sucher and I joined in for the fun. There were times that we had three different shows in rehearsal plus the daily class work. And I think we were all always available to be an "outside eye" for all student work. Susan was always up for driving into Madison to see a movie and have dinner locally. It was the best medicine for keeping cabin fever away.

The buildings and studios were beautiful. Meg redesigned a fabulous apartment over the Schoolhouse Studio. If you were as tall as Meg your arms were not always invited to dynamically vibrate to full extension over head but that was the only draw back. The studios would carry the sound of Tom singing Sur le Pont d'Avignon, Lotte Goslar, Lotte Goslar...

Everyone looked forward to the spring and summer when guest teachers would arrive. If you were fortunate, as I was, perhaps your destiny was altered forever. One summer I met William Burdick and it was at a time when my time at the studio was expiring – a little like a library card. If I were to land in New York, William invited me to be a part of his New York Renaissance Dance Company. And I did land in New York. I always said that William found me a place to live and a job. The only thing he didn't find for me was a husband. That I did "performing" as a waitress at one of the first outdoor seating restaurant/ cafes in New York. One always had a job besides teaching and performing in New York. And those were the good old days!

I had a wonderful career in New York and teaching at universities from 1978 to 1988. Reid and William were often a part of my jobs outside of New York. In 1991 I joined Tiffany & Co., a global luxury retailer in New York and had a second fabulous career and retired from the organization in June 2010 as the Director – Human Resources, Retail and Canada. I lived in New York and San Francisco and traveled throughout the US opening up new stores.

Chances are if a Tiffany store opened between 1997 and 2001 and as late as 2008 in certain markets, I had something to do with it. My theater discipline and performing experience was a definite asset in my work and my progressive career at Tiffany's. I was there for 18 years.

I remain united in marriage to the man I met at the restaurant in 1978, Paul Persoff. He is the professional webmaster for the Valley Studio website. We spend the best days together sharing interests in history, current politics, fine arts, performing arts, travel, Native American history, friends, wines and are asking the question-what are we going to do next? We share in a love and respect for mentors I have had – William Burdick and Reid Gilbert and the deep friendships that were made from my life in the arts and are still under cultivation.

So Many Memories

John Towsen

Getting picked up at the Madison airport by Joe Daly in that old bus. Tenting uphill from Ronlin Foreman and across the fence from a herd of cows. The Wisconsin Cheese Factory and Taliesen. Almost drowning in the Wisconsin River after smoking too much pot. William Burdick's smile, Peter Hoff's manic energy, Tom Leabhart's "Lotte Goslar, Lotte Goslar." Falling in and out of various stages of like, lust, and love. Hobart and the conch shell. Reid's grace and humor, Carlo's sparkling eyes. The House on the Rock (never visited); the Spring Green Restaurant (once); and Bob's House of Friends (countless times).

Over the course of three summers ('75, '77, '78) I spent a total of 18 weeks at the Valley Studio, and the experience was in many ways more formative for me than all of my long academic career. In fact, I'm in touch with more people from those days in Wisconsin than from my undergrad and grad days at NYU. The Valley Studio was a place to explore freely without looking over your shoulder. Maybe we were all having too much fun to worry about how good or bad we were at the 15 or 20 different performance styles we got to sample. I think a lot of us came away from there thinking we were onto something important, that what we were doing with our talents was good for us and good for the world. And we were right.

Tee pee, for Winter Togetherness

Champion Watermelon Seed Shooter

Ezekiel Peterhoff

Reid is a champion watermelon seed shooter: a master! He developed his skill over a lifetime. He could shoot a watermelon seed twenty feet and hit somebody's head with it. Then he'd sit there playing with his chopsticks like he didn't know nothin' about it. That happened plenty of times.

Pure genius with his timing and really skillful. Now he didn't spit it. He'd hold the seed in his fingers and squeeze them together and shoot it out that way: between the index finger and the thumb. He did it that way.

He was so impish about it. I'm sure he can still do it. People would be swatting mosquitos that didn't exist and lookin' around thinking "where'd that come from?" Reid's just sittin' there nonchalantly picking at his rice. Those Appalachian storytellers have control!

ZEKE, JOHN & THE TEEPEE

You remember the teepee, right? Well, me & John (Towsen) had a very memorable night in that teepee. We slept out there in that teepee with some girl. We laid there lined up like logs, the three of us, and we just laughed all night long. You know we went out there to escape, and it was bug infested, and you'd hear the deer outside and it sounded like bears. It was not gentle. It was like the Little Rascals in the spook house. We stayed out there all night and did nothing but laugh. I don't think I've laughed so much in my life.

GENERAL THOUGHTS ABOUT THE PLACE

You've got to remember that people would come to the Valley Studio, and they'd already be trained. They'd bring their stuff with them. They would already have learned some other aspect of movement theater. That's why Reid's choices of teachers was so good. He'd have people like Mamako and William (Burdick). If you'd come from being trained as a white-faced mime, you'd never have contact with someone like those two. You'd come to the Studio and you'd find something new, something that got you to grow and create something new for yourself. For the most part, people there knew what they were looking for: making and creating new stuff.

Many activities made the Valley Studio a place of magical balance where people worked close to their best potential. I remember in the summer we'd start every new session with stick dancing on the front lawn. It was the first event, maybe Sunday night before things really got started on Monday. We would go out and stick dance. There was a box of fourteen inch long heavy dowels. You'd hold a stick in each hand. You'd clap the sticks together, then you'd turn to the person next to you and clap the sticks over your head, left, right, left. Then clap yours together. Then turn to the person behind you.... I believe it was Reid's idea, but many of us would lead it from time to time. What a great way to get to know all the new people you'd be working with.

Addendum

Beyond the fun of the game, it helped us to develop a sense of personal timing and also to be able to coordinate one's personal movement in response to the rhythm of the others. The theatre too often has actors who have difficulty responding adequately with the rhythm of other performers.

erg

It Will Change Your Life

Ron Anderson

In the late 70s, I was an MFA acting student at the University of Georgia. I had become frustrated with academic theatre and wanted very much to train in mime. Narrowing my choices to Tony Montanaro's school in Maine and the Valley Studio in Wisconsin, I asked around for recommendations. Another grad student, Michelle Moraine, said she had been to the Studio for a summer and said I should choose it over the Celebration Barn. "You absolutely have got to meet Reid Gilbert and study with him. It will change your life."

So, I did. And it did.

In 1977, I came to the Studio for a summer intensive, studying illusion pantomime with Reid, corporeal with Tom Leabhart, puppetry with Robin Reed, and loved every minute of it. I came back the next summer, continued to work with Reid, and added dance with William Burdick and circus technique with Hovey Burgess. I fell in love with the place, the people and the process of creation that seemed to permeate the entire Wyoming Valley. I was so enamored in fact, that after Debbie and I got married in late summer 1978, I left my grad program at UGA, and we moved to Spring Green to became full-timers at the Studio. It did change my life. I have worked professionally as an actor, director and theatre teacher for almost 40 years, and I owe much of my love of, knowledge of and dedication to theatre to Reid Gilbert and his vision for the Studio as a genuine place for discovery.

In the summer of 1978, the Valley Studio staged a production of Euripides' *The Bacchae*, with William Burdick's brother Jacques directing. Jacques Burdick taught at Adelphi University, and he took classical theatre more than a little seriously. However, our production was not going particularly well, and Peter Hoff (Dionysus) and I (Pentheus) began clowning around in rehearsal. Jacques didn't seem to mind, and in fact rather enjoyed the lightheartedness of it. A fast and loose quality began to alter the process as we added juggling shtick to the interrogation scene. Recognizing that we were not just having fun, but serious about adding the bit to the show, Jacques said, "Wait a minute – I don't think we're sending up the play." A day or so later, we added fire torches to symbolize the destruction of Thebes, and he said, "Are we sending up the play?" Finally, when Peter showed up in a diaper with a big D on it, Jacques gave in and yelled, "All right then. Let's send up the play!!"

Our presentation of *The Bacchae* was by far the funniest and in some ways the most effective production I have ever witnessed. Almost everything was done in complete clowning and slapstick style, and the audience loved every minute of it. Slapstick that is until the Messenger's speech. Jacques wanted that speech played absolutely straight, and he even referred to it as dramatic relief. He was dead on – following so much silliness, the solemn but urgent nature of that speech stunned the audience, gave the play a breathtakingly dramatic turn, and beautifully set up the devastation that was to come. I was a part of the show, but I was also in awe of the show – and I will never forget that experience.

I learned a critical lesson from Jacques Burdick that summer, and have used it in my directing ever since. Honoring what's on the page is of course an important part of the production process. And having a definite directorial concept is equally important. But what happens in the rehearsal hall doesn't just compliment that work – it completes it. You only truly find the play in the rehearsal hall, and you must work with the cast you have. Drawing from the actors' strengths, encouraging their exploration and allowing them to be equal partners in the play's creation, not only produces a better ensemble spirit – it leads to a far more interesting and successful outcome than you could ever have envisioned otherwise.

Obsessed with Mime

Debbie Anderson

My husband, Ron, and I came to the Valley Studio from Athens, Georgia shortly after we were married in early fall 1978. He was obsessed with mime and wanted to leave his grad program at UGA, so that he could pursue mime full time. I was a musician with a degree on flute and a longtime love of singing. I didn't really know or care anything about mime, and I wasn't sure that leaving in the middle of his Master's program was smart, but I wanted to support Ron – so we moved to Wisconsin.

Ron studied full time at the Studio, and I took a few classes when I could. I will never forget taking a dance class with Angel Vigil. He was a very good teacher: thorough, patient and endearingly quirky. He called your butt the po-po, which I thought was cute, and he had a way to helping non-dancers actually understand terminology, posture and movement. One day, when he was trying to get me and my uncoordinated legs to comprehend *changement*, I finally said, "Oh, you mean swap feet!" He said, "Yes – that's exactly right," and he called it *swap feet* from then on.

To help pay for our stay at the Studio, I worked part-time as Ellen's assistant in the kitchen, and later became the full-time cook. I had learned from her to be sensitive to the needs and special requests of all the residents, and I became quite good at vegetarian cooking – which was brand new to me.

I remember one Saturday for lunch, we were simply having sandwiches and soup. I had made potato soup and fried just enough bacon for BLTs for the meat eaters in the group. (And I had counted very carefully.) However, about half way through the lunch line, several students asked me where the bacon was. I looked at the serving plate and while there was plenty of lettuce and tomato, there was no bacon left.

I went into the dining hall and asked, "Would you raise your hand if you had bacon on your sandwich?" God bless their honesty – I believe that every vegetarian in the room raised their hand.

Our Home at Valley Studio

Tom and Sally Leabhart

From 1976-78 we made our home at the Valley Studio. My first job after leaving Decroux's school in Paris (1968-72) was at the University of Arkansas. In the third year of my four years there, we attended the mime festival in Viterbo, Wisconsin, where we met Reid Gilbert for the first time. Inspired by the work of Ctibor Turba and Boleslav Polivka at the Mime Festival, and intrigued by Grotowski's writings and legend, we then spent three months in Poland and two months in Czechoslovakia on an International Research and Exchanges Board grant. One morning in Warsaw we received a letter from Reid at our hotel, asking if we wanted to come to Wisconsin to discuss a future collaboration.

When we got back to the US from Poland we visited the Valley Studio and met with Reid. At the time, Sally and I thought a move to the wilds of Wisconsin the most natural thing in the world, and as we look back on those years we cherish the great friendships made and the lessons learned in art and in life: wonderful communal meals and happy times washing up in the kitchen; walks under vast night skies along the dirt roads accompanied by Smokey the dog; "sharings" in which everyone brought a song, a story, or a theatre piece; unbelievably cold winter nights—-one night without heat when our cats slept as close to our faces as possible, trying to stay warm; trips into Madison in our yellow VW Bug to visit Ella's Delli and Paul's Books. When I look at photos from that time I realize what kids we were, not much older than our students.

Thinking back over the twists and turns of life's path, we're grateful for the good times in Spring Green, where we learned more than we taught and made friends for life.

Sally is a full-time Pilates teacher with clients in California and in France. Tom has taught for 32 years at Pomona College and gives workshops regularly in France and Spain.

Tom Leabhart, Corporal Mime Class

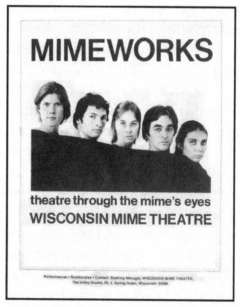

Mimeworks: Meg Partridge, James Van Eman,
Susan Chreitzberg, John Aden, Karen Flaherty

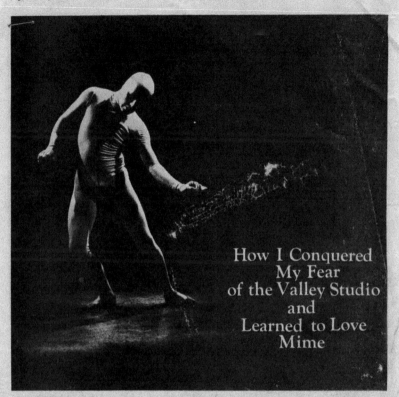

How I Conquered
My Fear
of the Valley Studio
and
Learned to Love
Mime

Photographs and Text by Gary Stallings   Title Photograph by Zane Williams

I've always been afraid of Valley Studio. They do something out there called
Mime. I don't know what Mime is. That's what always scared me. This guy in
the funny suit is Thomas Lebhart. He's one of the teachers. So you can imagine
what the students are like.

But I went out there anyway.

I found William Burdick teaching people to dance the way I dance in my dreams. I visited his class and wanted to stay there.

This is Jacque Burdick. He makes people sing. He doesn't teach them how; he just makes them do it. After fifteen minutes in his class, I was sure he could make me into a Caruso or a Crosby anytime he had a free afternoon.

Valley Studio Memories

Derry Graves

OFFICE MANAGER/COMMUNITY LIAISON
1977 – 1978

Mid-day July '78

A rehearsal/teaching session piece was being acted out on the small out-door wooden stage. Two actors (mimes) both in close fitting all white attire, from the top of the head to tip of the toe. Not white-faced. Perhaps Tom Leabhart was one of the two. The backdrop behind the stage and the two white-costumed mimes were completely covered in Queen Ann's lace, in full bloom. This white-on-white scene is well remembered by me. Very beautiful. On stage and off.

Another stage presentation was on the in-door theatre space. There were two performers both in white face, comedic masks and a park bench. It was the first time I had seen masked work. Since then I have so wished to see such material again. It was excellent.

Another stage setting. The grassy knoll above the office building and below the dorm/kitchen. Mary Jo Anderson was doing a piece wearing ordinary clothing, and needing a weapon. She used the spent dry stem of a day lily as her sword. I thought Mary Jo was a terrific actor with or without such a grand sword.

My Shangri La

Angel Vigil

The Valley Studio was a beautiful time in my life. I really do think of it as my own personal Shangri La – a remote, secluded, spiritual and artistic haven, presided over by a benevolent and caring teacher and mentor, Reid Gilbert.

The Valley Studio also represents the most wonderful memories of my youth. The soft patina of time makes all my memories of that time so filled with the promises of youth and the hopefulness that all was good in the world. The dearest memory is the one of who I was at that time as I was discovering and developing the sense that I was an artist on the beginning of a life long adventure as a creative person, an artist and educator.

I had cast my fate to the wind and I was on the way to Ann Arbor, Michigan, because I had heard that it was an interesting place with interesting people doing exciting things. Such a simple thought but it was enough to put me on the road. I was riding my Harley Davidson motorcycle across the country and the open road only promised adventure.

I had left Kansas City where I had been a dancer with the Kansas City Ballet and had dabbled in the miscellaneous performing arts of theatre, dance, mime and circus. I had also studied the martial arts and combined with my other activities I felt that I was pretty familiar with various forms of movement expression.

I had heard about the Valley Studio and decided to drop by and check it out on my way to Ann Arbor. My thoughts were no more developed than that. A casual decision to detour changed my life. One road ended and another revealed itself.

I walked up the gravel drive to the Valley Studio and was impressed by how quiet and beautiful the place was. And the buildings looked so unique. Only later did I learn that the special environment was styled after the design aesthetic of Frank Lloyd Wright.

I met Reid almost immediately and after a casual conversation I asked him if I could stay awhile and study. He took me up to a dance studio and asked me to show him what I could do. I remember I did a few simple mime/dance pieces I knew and talked with Reid a little more about what I was looking for.

I will always be thankful to the fates that they brought me Reid and the Valley Studio at the right time in my life. It really was an example of the familiar aphorisms – seek and you shall find, leap and the bridge will appear. Without even really knowing what I was looking for I had found it – an artistic home where I could learn, grow and develop. It was a springboard to a life-long path.

I had two different periods at the Valley Studio. The first and most intense was as a student. In the second period, equally fulfilling but in a different more measured way, I returned as a teacher after a summer performing with the Wisconsin Mime Theatre in Milwaukee. The memories of each period are powerful but I must admit that like most experiences in life nothing ever matches the first time for its startling and life changing effect. Like Rick and Ilsa in *Casablanca* who will always have Paris I will always have the memory of my first time at the Valley Studio. Heck it was where I discovered my all time favorite movie *Les Enfants du Paradis, The Children of Paradise.*

I know this all sounds so dramatic and overblown but as I look back over the decades of my life I now recognize that my time at Valley Studio was a most important and formative time of my life. I arrived unformed, young and immature. But I was a youthful wanderer who had gone into the world seeking my fortune and without even realizing it at the time I had found it.

So what did I find?

I found in Reid a teacher who was willing to give me a chance.

I will always see him as a kind mentor. He was the person who really gave me an opportunity to find myself.

I found gifted teachers who showed me what it was to live the artistic life. Three who remain especially memorable are Carlo Mazzone Clementi, Mamako Yoneyama and William Burdick. As I think back now I am amazed at the great good fortune I had to study with such world masters. And all because Reid created a place where he invited these incredible performers and teachers and gave students the opportunity to study and learn from them. What a gift!

I have distinct memories of many of the people I met at the Valley Studio. One night Randall Duk Kim came to the Valley Studio seeking support for a theatre he was starting in Spring Green, the American Players Theatre. Years later I saw him as the Keymaker in one of the Matrix movies.

I also had the good fortune to meet people passing through the Valley Studio who later went on to their own renown and accomplishments. Mary Jo Anderson became a movie and TV actress. Joe Martinez became an esteemed fight choreographer. John Towsen wrote the definitive history of clowning. John Russell set a Guinness World Record for stilt walking. Jim Calder established himself as an eminent actor, director and teacher in New York.

I even got to meet and spend time with the legendary Itinerant Fool Ken Feit. He softly challenged me to attend to my spiritual life and when I heard of his death years later I was thankful that my path had crossed his. And again all because of the Valley Studio.

I also found the most wonderful community of fellow students. I have the clearest memories of so many people. Special shout-outs have to go to my work buddy Carl, my performing partner Dennis Richards, my motorcycle partner Jim Van Enam who tore down the ZZ road at over 100 miles an hour with me, Nancy Lynner, Tanja Anselm, Roger and Nina, and Ron and Debbie Anderson. They and so many others have all remained in my memory over the years. We were all so young! What an amazing time of our lives! Living, laughing, loving and learning! It was fun!

I miss them all and that time and who I was in those days. There are so many specific intense memories of events and people that it would take pages to record them. I know one can never return to one's youth but to quote Bob Dylan my memories of the Valley Studio are forever young.

My enduring feeling about the Valley Studio is thankfulness. Thankfulness that Reid had the vision for an artistic center that would bring together kindred spirits from all over the world and then he went and created it. Thankfulness that he invited me into his artistic home. Thankfulness that I had the opportunity to study with such powerful artists. Thankfulness that I met so many good people and had the opportunity to share a special time in our lives with them.

And thankfulness that because of the Valley Studio I learned I could live my life as an artist.

Shangri La, the Elysian Fields, Camelot, Nirvana. All are magical and mythical places to nurture the human soul. But also imaginary like once upon a time and happily ever after.

Luckily for all of us who experienced it the Valley Studio was real and actually happened.

Even though the Valley Studio's time has passed I am reminded of a Dr. Seuss quote: "Don't cry because it's over. Smile because it happened."

The memory of Valley Studio is an eternal smile.

Addendum

As we were closing down Valley Studio due to financial difficulties, all those still there had a meeting concerning the place itself and our own personal destinies.

Sensing my anxiety, Angel said, "Reid, we mustn't focus on the negativity of closing down. We must celebrate the positive, affirming that Valley Studio did exist for us and many others for the time that it did"

That helped me deal with my grief.

erg

Valley Studio's Soul

Stanley Allan Sherman

Reid's gathering of mimes, clowns and storytellers in the middle of the United States somewhere. Reid was always gathering young, middle aged, experienced and those having a new sparkle in their eyes. When he visited in New York, he insisted we go out for Indian food and of course Reid knew the best place. There were about five of us. Reid took care of ordering. As the food was served and we started eating, Reid stopped us, insisting we use our fingers. Why? *"Because the fingers taste too. It is part of the eating experience. Americans lose this element of taste in their fingers."* We all dropped our silverware. We were now all eating with our fingers and got involved with our food more than we every had. Using the bread as a utensil, scooping up different textures with our fingers. Reid is right, the fingers taste too. Reid's giving of knowledge is similar; our involvement with our art needs to be complete. A complete total experience involving every part of our body and sharing. We are sharing, eating together at the same artistic table of creativity.

This was his Valley Studio. But Valley Studio did not end with Valley Studio. Valley Studio was Reid and it traveled where ever Reid Gilbert went. Putting together the Mime and Clown Festival in Ohio and other festivals, helping people out how ever he could.

Trust and sharing in people especially creative people was a major part of his life-long Valley Studio. Helping people come together. Turning people on to cultural, mime, clown, storytelling. Where ever I went in our country I would find a connection with

Reid. Performers that were at the beginning festivals Reid helped to create.

After the closing of Valley Studios, Reid Gilbert had a wealth of information and contacts, internationally. Valley Studios physically was no more. But when a fellow decided to start Movement Theater International, Reid gave all those contacts to Michael Pedretti. The continuing of sharing the bounty of food that was at the table which Reid started. And in a sense Valley Studio became Movement Theater International and we all went with it. When I was in Portland, Oregon with some of my political activist buddies, Ken Kesey was at a gathering at my friends John Platt's home. Ken Kesey talked about *the people's energy* and *how it goes horizontally not up and down vertically. With an organization, one of the healthiest things you can do is get out of the way and pass the mantel. Do not hang on to it, but let it go, grow and change.* This is exactly what Reid Gilbert did and Michael Pedretti took the mantel and did well. All the performers supported it and we performed, did workshops, took workshop connected, networked.

At one of these events, which Reid of course was at, I was speaking to a group of participants between events about the masks I was creating. Talking about an article I read in an old Drama Review in the 1970's about how in Bali their Balinese mask makers make two types of masks, those with souls and those without souls. The ones without they sell to the tourist, the ones with soul they use for their rituals. So I asked myself how does one put a soul in a mask? I figured it out. Well to everyone's shock – a man, a little older than most of us spoke up. *"I wrote that article. So happy to know that, not only did someone read it, it actually did some good."* This is all part of the sharing energy which Reid's Valley Studio created and continued.

At one of the many festivals he put together I received one of my favorite reviews. This was the OSU Ohio State University Mime and Clown Festival 1988. Here is my favorite quote of any review I have received and a link to the full review: http://www.maskarts.com/maskartsaeroshowreviews.htm

The Columbus Dispatch
Saturday July 9 1988

"Seriously, you must go see this clown

... Parents, take your kids! If you don't have any, that's no excuse. Borrow a few. Anyone who doesn't grab the whole family to see this weirdly wonderful fellow deserves to be arrested for criminal negligence. His show is that special. ..."

Reid and the Valley Studio energy allowed me to receive this review, just as Valley Studio helped so many others. A review like this, leads to paid bookings and helps any performer's livelihood. It also enabled this Ohio community to experience some very funny to hysterical performers for this Valley Studio Festival at OSU.

Just a few months ago I was contacted by Jean Barbou of The American Mime Theatre here in NYC; to repair some of their masks. Of course Jean and I started speaking and I mentioned Reid Gilbert's name and Valley Studio. Jean's face lit up! How is he ...? It was joy. Joy is what Reid Gilbert's Valley Studio is partly about and still living today thought everyone that passed through or was touched by this special total joy and sharing. The joyful soul of Valley Studio is still living.

Summer Homecoming

2011

Coming back to Wyoming Valley in 2011 was like a homecoming for me, as I had not spent an entire summer there since 1980, when my theatre and school (Valley Studio, Wisconsin Mime Theatre and School) closed.

Although I had written of the Valley before (A Sacred Valley), I had some premonition this was going to be an extraordinary return, because of several earlier happenstances.

Steven Wasson, a mime student of mine, left my school in 1976 to study in Paris with my teacher, Etienne Decroux, who was also Marcel Marceau's teacher. Steven and his wife, Corinne Soum, were the last assistants Decroux had before his death, and they carried on the mission of the school and moved it to London.

Three years earlier, after many years of being out of contact, he googled me and said that he felt it was about time for him to return to the Valley with his school. I told him to get in touch with Robert Graves, who with his wife, Derry, had brought me to the Valley in the mid-60s to teach and perform in the Uplands Arts Council summer programs.

Robert and Derry met Steven and Corinne and told them at that time that they didn't know of any available facility for a mime school. Shortly after that, the membership of the Wyoming Valley Methodist Church dwindled, and the church was put up for sale. Steven and Corinne bought the church and began refurbishing it. They even installed plumbing in the Ladies Hall, as there had never been more than an outdoor toilet at the church.

I had often reminded church congregations that the first verb in the bible is *created: "In the beginning God created . . ."* Continuing that thought, I also proposed that the creative act is also a spiritual act. The Wyoming Valley Methodist Church was continuing its spiritual mission in another form.

The Wyoming Valley School, designed by Frank Lloyd Wright (whose own Taliesin was only two miles away) was also abandoned and was donated to a non-profit organization as a cultural/educational center. It was only about a quarter of a mile up Route 23 from the church. Robert and Derry Graves provided leadership as well as maintenance and landscaping for that new re-newed venture.

The past January, Ron Baker, another former student of mine visited us in Tucson; the first time I had seen him since 1969, when I brought him to the Valley, along with several of his fellow students from Lambuth College, where I was teaching at the time. At the end of that summer he enrolled in the first theatre class at Juilliard.

I had heard that Ronnie had died, but learned differently three years ago when I attended the annual meeting at the Players Club in NYC. It is the annual setting of the honorary National Theatre Club, of which I'm their token mime. A new member, Stephen Henderson, said that he was in the first theatre class at Juilliard. After his introduction, I asked him if he knew Ron Baker. He assured me that he did and was greatly impressed with Ronnie's musical ability, particularly his singing the *Memphis Hollers.* When I asked him if it was true that Ron had died, he told me that Ron was alive and living in Los Angeles after a career of performing on Broadway, Off-Broadway, Off-Off-Broadway, San Diego Shakespeare Theatre and several films.

He also said that when he, himself, was just a youngster he had seen Ron perform in a little town in Wisconsin. I asked him if it was in Spring Green. He said, "Yes, it was Spring Green at the Gard Theatre in a production of *The Conversion of Buster Drumwright.*" I had directed the premiere of that script by Jesse Hill Ford in 1969 with Ron as the protagonist.

In Ron's January visit he said that he was working on a one-man show of Sam Houston because they were both from the same state, Tennessee, where Houston had been governor before he moved to Texas and became governor there. Ron was also intrigued by the fact that Houston was about the same size as he: 6'5", nearly 300 lbs and size 15 shoes.

I invited him to join me in the Valley in the summer, and I'd find a place for him to perform the premiere of his new show.

There was some difficulty in my finding a rental living space for the summer as both Taliesin and the American Players Theatre also had to find living quarters for their summer participants. For a while it looked as though I might be able to rent the apartment built for me in 1976 at the former mime school, but instead I found a place at Hilltop at the Quarry House, which in its former life had been the town hall of the Wyoming Valley Township. Herbert Fritz, a Frank Lloyd Wright associate architect, had bought the building many years ago, moved it to his farm, Hilltop, and renovated it for a residence. A dear friend of mine, Mary Stefansson, who had been on my office staff, had lived in the Quarry House for 37 years. The house was so named because it was situated in the farm's old quarry.

Herbert, now deceased, had been my architect at the mime school. It seemed to me that his architecture should be called, *Primitive Elegance.* I had participated in several of the rites of his family, officiating at the wedding of his son, Ty, and Janelle Chafee and four years later at the memorial service for their small daughter, Erowyn. It was, indeed, like coming home.

Although Steve Wasson, my former student and the new owner of the Wyoming Valley Church was not there for the summer, he had allowed local people to continue the monthly non-denominational hymn sings, which my business manager, Nina Edming, had started in 1975. I also had two evenings of storytelling events in the church, and it was in that church that Ron Baker premiered his script, *Houston.* Although Steve was not there for Ron's performance, he came the following Monday and these two students of mine (one from the 60s and one from the 70s) met for the first time.

The summer also afforded me the opportunity to hold a Sunday service at Unity Chapel, the home church of Frank Lloyd Wright's family. I had shared the Valley with Taliesin during the 70s, and this summer I was invited at formal night (special guests in formal evening wear) to perform in its Hillside Theatre after the dinner. I performed four short mime pieces and then demonstrated with kimono and mask how mime is used in the Japanese Theatre.

During all this time I saw my old friend, Robert Graves, several times, but his health seemed to be deteriorating even though he continued when able to work on landscaping at the Wyoming Valley School of which he was president of the board. Every summer Thursday evening in Spring Green the community holds what they call "Local Night" in a small park in the middle of town. Live music is performed on a small stage, and food and drinks are available. One evening two of my daughters came out from Madison for Local Night, and it was one of the few times that Robert and Derry were there. Later my daughters and Robert and Derry had said how very fortunate they had been to make that connection that evening.

On the last day I was there I went by the Graves's to leave a copy of a rough draft I had written for a grant for the Wyoming Valley School. Derry, Robert and I sat on their veranda facng the ridge across the creek. When I left, knowing that I would be leaving the next day for Arizona, Robert, while still seated, gave me his usual hug and said, "It's always difficult saying goodbye to you, Reid." and I realized that there was a more consequential message than usual from him.

The next day I left the Valley for a two-day driving trek back to Arizona with Clayton, my grandson. It was a wonderful, though fast-paced trip, and we learned a lot about each other ... learned a great deal more than we would ever have learned if we had not been confined in a metal cage, hurtling sometimes at eighty – five miles an hour across the Great Plains.

After settling back into the rhythms of home in Tucson, having been away for three months, Tia, one of Robert and Derry's daughters phoned and said that her dad was fading fast, as they were told it would be only a few days until his passing. She asked me if I would be able to conduct his memorial service, which he had requested. I, of course, agreed even though it would be extremely difficult as Robert had been like a brother to me for more than half a century. She called again on Labor Day, saying that Robert had passed away that morning with his wife, son and four daughters with him.

Barbara and I began making airline arrangements to return to the Valley and were able to get the Quarry House at Hilltop for the few days, even though it had already been rented to someone else.

The service was held in the same church, the Wyoming Valley Methodist Church, which my student had bought ... the church where Robert's parents were leaders and where Robert and his siblings, as well as his children, had attended church and Sunday school, so many years earlier...and where I had officiated at the wedding for my daughter, Karen. The reception after Robert's memorial service was to be just up the road at the Wyoming Valley School, where Robert and Derry had labored during the summer to get it ready for classes and performances.

Robert had requested of Derry that I lead the attendees in singing AMAZING GRACE the way my grandfather had sung it in Spoon Creek Primitive Baptist Church. That method was *a capella,* but with the leader reciting a line, immediately followed by the whole gathering singing the line. This rhythm is maintained throughout the singing of the song.

The shared singing was a fitting farewell to Robert.

I will not attempt to relate for the current reader my remarks, except to include here a poem I wrote, inspired by Robert's life and to include the benediction at the end of the service:

DEATH IS MORE

Death is more than passing over.
though it is that and much more.
It is a cessation of shared work and play
as we have enjoyed so oft before.
But there will be times in days ahead
when those of us left here behind
will remember past times of joy
vividly bringing those moments to mind.
There will be occasions in the days ahead
when great wisdom will be received
by the ones on this side of the mysterious door,
as spoken directly by the one gone before.
And as we lay to rest the mortal frame
may we be comforted by memories of his life,
and now embracing each other in his name
be comforted in our present joy or strife.

"Now cracks a noble heart. Goodnight, sweet prince, and flights
of angels sing thee to thy rest."
Go now in peace and may the peace and love which passeth
understanding go with you now and in the days ahead. Amen

It was truly a celebrational homecoming and a grief-filled parting!
E. Reid Gilbert
September 14, 2011

P.S. Robert's memorial service was the last non-theatre event
in the building that was to become a different kind of creative
celebration; appropriate indeed for this man who served as the link
between the tradition of Christian worship in the Wyoming Valley
Methodist Church and the new White Church Theatre Project of
the *Theatre de l'Ange Fou.*

My Road to the Valley Studio

Steve Wasson

On this sun filled, late spring day, I am sitting in my theatre, the White Church Theatre Project, putting down some impressions of my time at the Valley Studio. Nearly forty years have gone by since I was a student at Reid Gilbert's utopian adventure in the forested hills of southwestern Wisconsin, and now, strange destiny that I have, I find myself back in those hills with a theatre in an old church just a mile from where I began my study of mime and physical theatre. My road to, and away from, and finally back to this haunted valley, this lost paradise, is the stuff of dreams. So, backtrack I must to try and weave a short tale of this road.

In January 1970, as a young literature student in Colorado, I was talked into helping a few friends audition for a play, and sang a few lines to an unknown song and went home. In the morning I saw one of them and asked how the audition went for him. He said, "Nothing for me, but they want you!" Thinking there must be a mistake, I went to the cast meeting and, before I could pull out of the predicament, I found myself doing a read-through of Alfred Jarry's "Ubu Roi", and volunteering to play every role. I ended up doing around 9 or 10 of the smaller roles from the sword-fighting prince to a series of beheaded royalists.

My heart was hooked. So, this was theatre: imagination and movement and daring, the cubist dance of Chaplin, of Keaton, the absurdist world of the Marx Brothers, the swashbuckling of Errol Flynn, a realm of athletic poetry...or so I thought. And after a year of disappointing theatre classes, I quit the university to work in a steel mill and ponder over what to do with my life.

During these wandering years, I began to ask myself, how does one become something like a Chaplin or Keaton today? Vaudeville was long gone, the music hall a memory.

And then one day in March 1975, while sweeping endless dust next to the world's largest electric steel furnace, the revelation came to me to go to India. I had been studying and following the teachings of the "Avatar of the Age" Meher Baba since I was 18, and maybe in the atmosphere of India I would figure a few things out.

India was all and so much more than I could have thought I wanted. Meher Baba's disciples were very supportive, and a few close ones even suggested I do something like studying mime, move to Paris, doing something different in theatre.

Back in the states, I wrote to a newspaper in Illinois, to an advice column. I asked, "Where does someone study mime?" A week later they answered, "Here is the address of Marceau's agent in New York, but there is another place which you might look into. The Valley Studio, outside of Spring Green, Wisconsin, is the home of the Wisconsin Mime Theatre and school, directed by Reid Gilbert."

I went to the Valley Studio in December 1975 to audition. Driving through a blizzard, I arrived the night before and rented a motel room. Nervous as could be, I couldn't sleep, so I moved the furniture out of the way and rehearsed my audition piece all night long.

As I arrived at the studio, exhausted, at 8am, Reid Gilbert showed me to a small, unheated rehearsal room in the barn. And there I performed my little masterpiece for him. He just watched with his head tilted back a bit, and when I finished, told me what I could have done here or there. He asked me why I wanted to study at his school and I told him, "I would like to learn the craft of acting." Reid laughed, and said, "Welcome to the Valley Studio."

Back to the steel mill for a few more months, I saved what I could; found a small house for my two dogs and me. And then on Friday, February 26, I worked my last shift in the mill. On Monday,

March 1, 1976, at 9am, I was in my first mime class, lying on my back along with the other students, after a warm up with two company members, Kaye Potter and John Aden. Eyes closed and wondering what was next, I heard a door open and footsteps crossing the floor. Then came Reid's voice, "The movement is coming from the inside, like a hand in a glove..."

The Valley Studio was a unique place. In the heart of Frank Lloyd Wright country, hidden away on a gravel road was this cluster of old and new buildings: A one room school house used for mime and dance classes, the barn studio and costume shop with company member's apartments, the farm house and office, the new Wright apprentice designed 'lounge' where many classes and events were held and, connected to this, the dormitory for the students living on the site and the great dining hall. All of this surrounded by the forest and rolling hills of the Wyoming Valley, seemed an idyllic setting for a centre dedicated to creating a new form of theatre. The atmosphere was very far away from the academic machine of the university. The apprentice program students were from around the US, some with theatre backgrounds, and many drawn to discover something different.

This uniqueness of the Valley Studio was spread out over many levels. The classes emphasized personal creativity. Every mime class was steeped in improvisation. A subject was given and away we would go. Solos became duets and then ensemble work. And we were performing whenever the opportunity came. It was learning through experience. There was much talk and discussion amongst the apprentices of Marceau, Lecoq and the enigmatic Etienne Decroux. Within the first week I was introduced to the two Parisian schools with a show we attended by Mummenschanz from the Lecoq school, and a viewing of "Les Enfants du Paradis" with Jean Louis Barrault and Etienne Decroux.

Reid would often talk of his time studying with Etienne Decroux. One day in class, after an improvisation, Reid told me, "It is good, but what you need is more technique." I heard this a number of times, and then finally asked him, "What do you mean by technique? I understand a technique in music or dance or this or that, but what is a technique in mime?" He looked at me for a moment and then said, "We will start a technique class every day." And that is how I became introduced to corporeal mime and the artistic world of Decroux. Very soon, Reid brought in Tom Leabhart, an ex-assistant of the French master, to reinforce this direction.

The summers at the Valley Studio were different: Guest artists and teachers were coming and going, the number of students swelled to fifty or more, the myriad of classes, presentations, discussions and social encounters resembled a summer long celebration.

In the two and a half years there, I studied mime, ballet, voice, performed in a travelling commedia troupe, worked in a radio broadcast, did comic fashion shows, directed my first work, and played in 3 independent films by William "Dom" Robinson.

What I learned and absorbed in this time fired up in me the desire to experience what I felt to be the source. Etienne Decroux was to become the most important artistic influence in my life, and I eventually left for Paris to study with him.

It was in Decroux's school in the Parisian suburb of Boulogne-Billancourt that I met my life partner, Corinne Soum. We married in 1981 and then a little later were asked by Decroux to become his assistants. This privileged position, living in his home, taking care of practical things around the house along with teaching classes, and rehearsing with him was intense and enriching. Decroux created four new pieces on us, and re-worked some of his older work for us.

Being the last assistants of the master of mime, we were fortunate to receive in abundance the fruit of his sixty-year career. And with all of this, we eventually started our own school, the Ecole de Mime Corporel Dramatique (later becoming The International School of Corporeal Mime), and our company, the Theatre de l'Ange Fou.

And so began a voyage of over 30 years in Paris and London, performing around the world and teaching to numerous students. With the Theatre de l'Ange Fou and school, we have created some 40 original plays, directed other theatre groups, and had the privilege to work with the Royal Shakespeare Company's production of "Les Enfants du Paradis". We also did the first ever reconstruction of the major work of Etienne Decroux with "The Man Who Preferred to Stand" in 1992, premiered in Philadelphia and toured throughout Europe. Then in 2010, Corinne and I purchased the old Wyoming Valley Church outside of `Spring Green, Wisconsin turning it into a theatre for mime and physical theatre, the White Church Theatre Project. And this is where we are now. From Spring Green to Paris to London to Spring Green, back to the where I started, and now continue.

The Valley Studio was truly a utopian idea, and despite its relatively short life span, was an unforgettable undertaking. Reid was and is an 'homme de songe', man of the daydream, as Decroux would have put it. Reid Gilbert, this visionary poet, mime, director and teacher and his Valley Studio opened the door for me to dare to pursue my dreams, or as Etienne Decroux said, "make visible the invisible."

Addendum

At one of his evening lectures when I was studying with him in NY, Decroux said, "It's okay to whittle an 18inch wooden figurine. (I had recently whittled such a figurine.) But you haven't made your dramatic statement, until you've attacked a 20-ton boulder of granite with a chisel and sledge hammer."

I can affirm that Steven and Corinne are chiseling away at the 20-ton boulder of granite, as they perform major cultural epics and myths.

erg

Theatre de l'Ange Fou, "The Orpheus Complex"
created and directed by Steven Wasson.

About the Compilers

E. REID GILBERT

Before Valley Studio, Reid had pursued education with degrees from five colleges, culminating with a PhD in Asian Theatre. He served several years in the Methodist and Unitarian ministries. Teaching theatre in small colleges before VS, he then taught at Ohio State University from where he retired as Professor-Emeritus. Since then he directed a repertory theatre in West Virginia for ten years. Since then he has been writing theatre scripts and film scripts and has published five books. He claims his next book will be titled LIFE BEGINS AT 40 + 40.

JEF LAMBDIN

After studying with William Burdick and Peter Hoff at the Valley Studio in 1978, Jef returned to his work with North Carolina's touring mime theater, TOUCH. He created and performed with TOUCH until 1993, when the troupe was dissolved. He then worked for the Durham Bulls Baseball Club creating and performing as their mascot, Wool E. Bull, until 1997. Since then he's been performing at fairs and festivals as The InterACTive Theater of Jef, and sharing arts education residencies throughout the Southeastern U.S.

CPSIA information can be obtained
at www.ICGtesting.com
Printed in the USA
FSHW02n1316060618
49120FS